THE ART OF FRUGAL HEDONISM

A guide to spending less while enjoying everything more

THE ART OF FRUGAL HEDONISM

A guide to spending less while enjoying everything more

ANNIE RASER-ROWLAND WITH ADAM GRUBB

National Library of Australia
Cataloguing-in-Publication entry
Creator: Raser-Rowland, Annie, author
Title: The Art of Frugal Hedonism: a guide to spending less while enjoying everything more
ISBN: 9780994392817 (paperback)

Subjects:
Ethics of Consumption
Home economics—Accounting
Quality of life
Simplicity
Attitude change
Other Creators/Contributors: Grubb, Adam, author
Number: 178

Cover image by Marc Martin
Design by Adam Grubb
Publishing team: Meg Ulman, Su Dennett, Richard Telford and Ian Robertson
Printed in Australia by Focus Print Group Melbourne

This book is printed on paper using fibre supplied from plantation or sustainably managed forests.

First published by Melliodora Publishing 2016

Melliodora Publishing
16 Fourteenth Street,
Hepburn Victoria 3461, Australia
www.melliodora.com

Acknowledgements

Our thanks to our many interviewees: Su Dennett, Belinda Kerrison, Lawrence Hamilton, Isobel Harper, Danny Renehan, Meg Ulman, Patrick Jones, Srinath Baba, Peter Lalor, Joh M., Jack and Lois Monaghan, Trish Harris, Ibby E. Okinyi, and Nadia Faragaab.

Gratitude also goes out to the many people who gave feedback on sections of the manuscript as it evolved. Davina, Danny, Lucy, Sam, Hermann, Brooke, Nan, Marilyn, Taryn, Saskia, Shultz, Michael, and especially Frances Rowland, who read and re-read and gave reams of detailed and useful advice (and stayed gracious even when it was blithely ignored).

CONTENTS

FOREWORD Clive Hamilton

WHAT A TERRIFIC IDEA, a book showing how frugal living can be pleasurable. Not the kind of smug pleasure of the drop-out or the feeling of moral superiority that comes with driving a Prius (yes, that's me), but real actual sensual pleasure.

Critics of consumerism often talk about our 'addiction' to things, and it's a good way to think about it. Once you are hooked it takes over your life – you do crazy things to feed your addiction (like work incessantly, sacrifice relationships and run up debts), and yet the last hit doesn't really satisfy so you crave more.

Think about it: What would happen if all forms of electronic communication crashed overnight – no mobile phones, no text messaging, no Facebook, no email, nothing for the kids to watch on their iPads when having a 'family dinner' with their parents. Would people be unhappy? You bet they would. There would be screams of outrage, howls of distress, heart palpitations and demands that the government fix it quick.

But after a few days, a few weeks for the real addicts, people would find that there are other things to do, other ways to communicate (conversation is good). After all, in the 1950s – hell, in the 1980s – none of these things existed. Were people miserable then? In fact, all of the data show that people in the 1950s were happier! They had fridges but no air travel, telephones but no iPhones, pets but no pet jewellery, barbecues but no $7000 outdoor kitchens, and fast food that meant fish and chips.

Yet we have been convinced, not least by a vast marketing industry devoted specifically to the purpose, that we will be happy only if we have the latest gadget, a bigger house, a car that parks itself or a TV that swivels to face us if we shift from one end of the couch to the other. After all, the advertising industry exists to make us feel dissatisfied so that we buy more stuff.

In recent times marketing has zeroed in on one big message: Buying this thing or that thing will set you free. Cars, exotic holidays, insurance, home appliances, you name it; all of these things can liberate us, although they rarely say from what. The truth is that as long as we fall for these messages (and nearly all of us do) we are locked in a prison, the prison of consumerism, and that's the one prison that the marketers can never, ever promise to free us from.

When I look around it's pretty obvious who are the freest people in our communities – the ones who have escaped the prison of consumerism and money-hunger. They don't necessarily live in huts and go dumpster diving every night, but they manage to live self-possessed enjoyable lives with great friends and jobs they love. They do many things consumers do, but always in moderation (while occasionally lashing out, just for the hell of it). They eat well, stay fairly fit, give more, are socially engaged and stress less than most of us.

Bastards!

In fact, the freest and most contented people pretty much follow the advice in *The Art of Frugal Hedonism*.

Despite all of its pleasures, there is a downside to the kind of frugal living described in this book. If you practise it, some of your friends, family and colleagues will become cranky with you. They will tell you (or tell each other) that you are moralizing, putting yourself on a higher ethical plane. It doesn't matter how low key you play it, the chances are they will still load you up with these accusations. The truth is that they are not cranky with you; they are cranky with themselves.

In this situation there are two solutions – find new friends, family and colleagues, or slip them a copy of *The Art of Frugal Hedonism*.

———

Clive Hamilton is the author of *Growth Fetish* and co-author with Richard Denniss of *Affluenza: When Too Much Is Never Enough*.

ABOUT THIS BOOK

DEAR READER,

We want you to have an excellent life. And we don't think you should have to spend much money to do it. This book is about how.

That doesn't mean pages of advice on collecting discount coupons, squirreling away soap ends, and constructing careful budgeting strategies, because:

a) Those things don't get to the heart of the relationship between how much you enjoy life and how you use money,

b) Your authors find those things dull to think about for very long, and certainly didn't want to spend two years writing a book about them.

Instead, this book provides a selection of tips that dive right into the soft gooey centre of *how we approach feeling good*, and how *that* affects our spending. It examines ways to overhaul some habits that you may have accidentally fallen into via living in a culture that encourages consumption at every turn. It looks at how changing those habits can generate a life that both makes more sense, and indulges your senses. There are some practical bits, and some science-y bits. There are some recipes, and some psychology. There are some serious bits, and some really quite preposterous bits…

About you

It doesn't matter how much money you have. This book is designed to be read by *anyone* interested in how consuming less can make life more magnificent. Or just anyone curious about how skilled cheapskates get away with it. You'll find it particularly useful if:

~ You're not sure that your current spending habits are shaping a life you really believe in.

~ You suspect that some of your consumption is having unpleasant side effects on your wellbeing.

~ You can enjoy the simplest things, but feel that spending money in certain ways is almost obligatory if you want to be a fully-fledged member of society.

~ You feel like the amount of paid work you need to do doesn't leave enough time or energy for the rest of life.

~ You recognize how lucky you are to live in a society of such material abundance and convenience as to have been unimaginable for most of human history…

~ …but you also sometimes feel overwhelmed by the endless choice and expectation that such a society brings. And confused that almost everything you're supposed to do to take part in modern life is increasingly acknowledged to be simultaneously sabotaging the very future of the planet as we know it. Dang.

If you are still trying to figure out what to do with these feelings, let this book be your primer for a life less dependent on the comforts of consumption, and more focussed on extracting maximum pleasure from the most essential parts of being human.

If you've already started changing your life in reaction to these feelings, let this book be your companion in forging an existence rich with pleasures both deep and cheap. Let it add to your box of tricks for living frugally but fantastically. Let it be there for you when you feel that your resolve to live like that needs a pep talk. Or just whenever you need a charming and erudite little book (modest cough!) to help you win your less frugal friends over to your way of doing things.

About frugality and hedonism

Frugality is commonly seen as the domain of the hair-shirt martyr, not to be entertained by any sane person who can afford all that Nice Stuff there is to buy. Your authors would like to demur. One of our biggest motivations for being frugal is hedonism.

> hedonism /ˈhēdnˌizəm/ the pursuit of or devotion to pleasure, especially to the pleasures of the senses.

This devotion can come in many forms however, and worshipping too fervently at the altar of *consumer* hedonism can really stuff you up for all the other kinds.

Which is where frugality comes in. The truly savvy hedonist avoids blunting her capacity for pleasure against a barrage of constant stimulation. He knows that the rewards of the journey frequently trump instant gratification. She shuns that level of convenience and indulgence that insidiously erodes her mental and physical vigour. He makes non-monetised sources of pleasure his first port of call, so that he's not trapped into shaping his life around earning. Far from being acts of martyrdom, such frugality-compatible behaviours can in fact be your best ticket to enjoying everything more on both the deeply fulfilling *and* sensually satisfying levels.

It takes some practice to become a 'frugal hedonist'. If you're used to pressing a button that says 'cheese' and having cheese come out, you might feel disgruntled about having to walk to the cheese mountain and exchange pleasantries with the cheese miners before you get your cheese. But imagine how much better that cheese will taste! Not to mention other perks, like your toned calves, the beautiful scenery on the way to the mountain, and your jovial friendship with a crew of talented cheese miners. Which is what Frugal Hedonism is all about: perceiving a more multidimensional spectrum of pleasures, and living accordingly.

About your authors

We both grew up as vaguely middle-class kids, which in the 1970s and 80s meant something a lot more frugal than it does now. More dirt, fewer screens, next to no takeaway meals, more walking to school, parents with bigger hair.

Reflecting on her teenage years, your author Annie recognises that she was already exhibiting unusual attitudes towards extravagance. She recalls a certain afternoon in her first sharehouse. She had just completed high school, and was working the five a.m. shift in a plastics recycling factory. Every day for a week she had packed a change of clothes to put on after finishing work, each item the same shade of furious cobalt blue, each sourced from various missions to second-hand stores. She would emerge from the factory into the midday West Australian summer sun, and walk through the industrial precinct to the ocean, where she would enter a rapture at her ability to merge via camouflage into the huge blue sky and the ocean that reflected it. On the final day of the week the recycling line turned up a cobalt blue wading pool shaped like a clamshell. She hauled it home on the train, and spent the afternoon gleefully ensconced in it amidst the overgrown, silvered grass of her backyard. While clinking the ice cubes in her glass of blue cordial, she gazed at the sky, trying to dissolve any sense of her own existence. She remembers thinking: "This is definitely the pinnacle of debauchery."

Your co-author Adam recalls being quite clear as a child that toasted sandwiches cooked over the fire were better than any other kind of dinner. His enthusiasm for cheap pleasures was confirmed when his parents got better jobs, and the family moved house. He missed their dilapidated old farm house dreadfully, and wasn't at all impressed with the sterile expensive new house that smelt of paint, though of course he soon found a bog down the road to go catch frogs in, so things were okay after all. Later, when his adolescent corneas went oblong, he insisted on getting the cheapest 'pensioner' glasses the optometrist had in stock, refusing his parents' offers of more fashionable frames. He also never once thought of asking for a car as a graduation present.

About your authors and this book

As we grew older, dear reader, your authors noticed that a lot of people in our unbelievably affluent society were struggling to thoroughly enjoy life, despite having it so good. Increasingly, those people were us – notwithstanding our promising starts. We pledged to not have a bar of it. We would nip this trend in the bud. If there was a tricky trap to avoid, we would avoid it! If there was banal brainwashing to buck, we would buck it! We wanted to live large! We wanted to stay healthy, curious, and alive to pleasure! And we wanted to do it without spending lots of money. Gradually, we became adept enough at it that people started asking us questions like this:

Q. Hello. Could you please tell me how you manage to work so little, and do so much cool stuff?

Q. What the hell is your secret? You should come over sometime and give me some ideas about how to spend less money. I'll make you risotto.

Q. How much money do you actually spend in an average week?

(We feel it's only polite to respond to this one here, as it doesn't come up elsewhere in the book: About AU$105 a week each, including bills but excluding rent/mortgage payments. The average Australian equivalent figure is AU$440 per person. It would be higher again if only adults were counted when calculating this average.)

Q. Why don't you guys write a book about how to live frugally and still have an excellent life?

So here we are. To get here, we surveyed the habits of our best Frugal Hedonist friends and wrote them down. We sought out people who grew up in cultures or eras that were better at turning resources into happiness than ours is and we captured their words in our dictaphone. We made a decoction of what we learnt, drizzled it over some fascinating facts and figures, and swirled the lot through our own favourite strategies for living ludicrously well while spending very little. We present the results here for your delectation.

1. CREATE YOUR OWN NORMAL

IT'S A WINTERY TUESDAY MORNING, and Family R's alarm clock is going off. Mr and Mrs R reluctantly extricate themselves from their sleepy spooning, and go rouse their two boys. They switch on the central heating, scramble through hot showers, electric shaves and hair blow-drys, and into freshly laundered clothes. They make coffee in the Nespresso machine, grab juice and milk from the refrigerator and slosh it into glasses and over cereal. Mrs R loads the work folders she optimistically brought home with her last night into the hatchback and heads off to the office. She stops for an extra takeaway coffee on the way, because she had a sweaty and restless night until waking at 4am to realise that the electric blanket was still on.

It's school holidays, and since Mr R works weekends and has Tuesdays off, he packs the kids into the station wagon and they head out to the cinema to see the latest animation blockbuster. They're halfway there when they realise that the younger boy has left his favourite toy at home. To avoid tears, they drive back to get it, which starts the older boy calling his little brother a "stupid baby". Mr R creates a swift distraction by announcing that after the movie they'll go buy the new computer game the older boy has been talking about all week. To ensure peaceable snack consumption, each kid gets his own popcorn, fizzy drink and candy for the movie. Mr R isn't hungry, but feels a bit glum that his one day off has been swallowed by child care, and buys himself an extra large popcorn and an icecream as consolation. After the movie they go to the toy store as promised, but the store is out of stock of the game, so they drive across town to check if another store has it. It doesn't, so each of the kids gets to choose something else to make up for the disappointment.

Mr and Mrs R had agreed that morning that there should be no takeaway lunches that day, given all the leftover potato salad and lamb roast from Friday night that needs eating. But by the time they leave the second toy store, the kids are pleading starvation, so they stop for pizza. The 'All You Can Eat' option costs hardly more than just ordering off the menu, so they choose that. Dad feels uncomfortably full by the time he gets up to pay, and the younger kid obviously had eyes bigger than his stomach, because as the heating in the car starts to make things stuffy, he vomits up ice cream and chocolate sauce all over himself. By the time they reach home and get his soiled clothes into the washing machine, it's already late afternoon and Mr R realises he hasn't even bought the new dog bed he'd meant to get to replace Fido's increasingly tatty-looking one. The kids watch a DVD in their room, and Mr R puts the clothes through the dryer, and stacks the dishwasher with the breakfast dishes. He then goes online to book the family's flights to Sydney for Mrs R's sister's 40th on the weekend, and waits for his wife to get home so he can head off to the gym, and also buy that dog bed on the way back.

Mrs R forgets her promise to come straight home, and stops off for some shopping, picking up some kids' underwear multipacks that are on special, and accidentally blowing more than she has earned so far that week on a beautiful silk skirt. She's not sure when she would wear it, and knows she needs to lose a little bit of weight for it to fit nicely, but it is just so gorgeous. Because of her late return, Mr R takes off to the gym so hastily that he forgets his training shoes. He doesn't feel like turning back, and decides to just buy a new pair on the way – he figures he probably deserves an upgrade anyway given how well he's been sticking to his exercise schedule. After working out he grabs an electrolyte drink and protein bar, and heads home. Everyone is pretty tired, so they decide to order Thai takeaway for dinner (binning the rest of the lamb roast), crank the heating up, and settle in for a cosy evening of TV.

WOULD YOU CONSIDER THIS DAY to be one of luxury? Family R certainly didn't feel like they were living The High Life – or even a particularly satisfying life – on the day described. They were just trying to get through another day in a way that hundreds of millions of people would rate as *normal*.

Yet two hundred years ago, the amount of resources that each member of Family R consumed on this day would have been impossible for the average human to match, and challenging even for popes and kings. Looking just at energy use, even as recently as the 1950s, a family of a similar socio-economic standing would have used *less than half* this amount on a typical day.

	IN 1950	NOWISH (2000/2010S)
AVERAGE HOUSE SPACE PER PERSON	27 m^2	83 m^2
PERCENTAGE OF HOUSEHOLDS WITH ONLY ONE OCCUPANT	10%	25%
ANNUAL DISTANCE TRAVELLED IN ROAD VEHICLES PER PERSON	4,900 km	16,200 km
PERCENTAGE OF FOOD PREPARED AT HOME	75%	50%
PERCENTAGE OF HOUSES WITH AIR CONDITIONING	10%	87%
TYPICAL SERVING SIZE OF POPCORN AT THE MOVIES	3 cups	16 cups!
HOUSEHOLD DEBT (AS A PROPORTION OF ANNUAL HOUSEHOLD INCOME)	50%-ish	200%-ish

Some stats from the U.S for your contemplation. And before you get too cocky other-English-speaking-countries, your figures don't look much better.

Miraculously, those middle class 1950s folk weren't spending their waking hours bemoaning this agonising deprivation – they felt just as normal as Family R do today. In fact, there is American research suggesting that its 1950s' citizens rated themselves as happier than its modern ones do.

Such contrasts illustrate just how much our concepts of 'wealth' and 'appropriate consumption' are defined by comparing ourselves to those around us. Even those of us who least identify with the phrase 'keeping up with the Joneses' can't help but measure ourselves against a hazy benchmark based on what our peers are doing, and what popular (and social) media *suggest* people are doing.

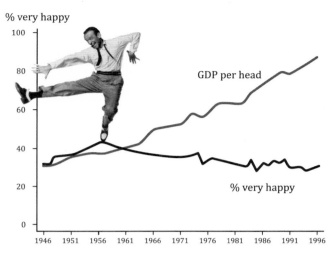

Increasing income and declining happiness in the USA,
known as the Easterlin paradox.

Consider again the kind of shifts in consumption we've highlighted above. Your pragmatic authors certainly don't bring them up so that we can all lash ourselves into a lather of personal and cultural guilt. Far from it. We mention them because we think there's something marvellously liberating (!) about acknowledging the total arbitrariness of what is considered 'normal' – it essentially clears the slate for us to make up our *own* normal. Suddenly we become free to do the tango on that slate, manoeuvring ourselves brazenly wherever our Frugal Hedonist supersenses may lead us…

Dearest reader, can you feel The Exceedingly Relative Nature of Things allowing you to regard the whole notion of 'normal' with more audacity, humour and philosophical perspective? If so, then we're all together on the dancefloor of infinite potential. It's time to boogie.

2. RELISH

'RELISH' IS A WORD WORTH MUSING UPON. It can sound almost indecent, with its suggestion of immoderate sensory intensity. Your authors regard this full engagement with the pleasure potential of life as the very finest skill in our frugality armoury.

We humans are ripe with nerve endings. Why waste them? Your author Annie remembers being a kid running around the bulk foods store with her best friend, plunging arms into the giant bins of dry beans and rating the different varieties for how fun they were for arm-plunging. She seems to recall that the kidney beans won, and while it is possible that you might be asked to take your business elsewhere if you try this as an adult, it does serve to illustrate how thickly strewn our daily lives are with sensual delights just begging to be noticed.

If you are walking home on one of those scorched afternoons where the heat is shimmering and your muscles are all warm and loose and the air is heavy with eucalyptus oils being baked out of the street trees, you might as well choose to enjoy all that sensory information coming at you like a molten sledgehammer. Sound challenging? Try this trick: treat it as if you'd *paid* for the experience and all its sensory elements. Soak it up with relish, and notice that you do not have to buy something to actively consume it.

Smack your lips and make appreciative noises when you're eating something tasty. Half-close your eyes when a sea breeze nips at the little hairs on the back of your neck. Stroke your dog's ear between thumb and forefinger and marvel at its silkiness. Snuggle into your bed on a cold night and actually grin about how good it is. Gaze at twinkly water until you feel a bit tipsy. Enjoy the rocking movement of the train. Go for a barefoot walk somewhere where you can curl your toes into brittle grass, mud or sand. Listen to music while doing nothing else at all. Call it mindfulness, call it living in the moment, call it relishing – it's recommended by psychiatrists, hedonists, Buddhist monks and cheapskates alike.

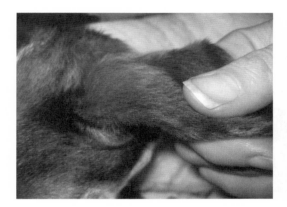 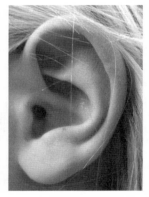

Stroke your dog's ear between thumb and forefinger and marvel at its silkiness...
Human earlobes also good.

What are some of the free or cheap things you're already relishing? Afternoon naps? Singing? Learning about colonial Australia's bushranger culture? Could you spend more time doing these things, or give yourself more space to really engage with them?

Conversation is surely one of life's greatest free relishables, and is certainly worth devoting time to. It too benefits from fuller engagement – people become more conversationally nimble and generous when they fully immerse themselves in the pleasure of talk. Help this happen simply by putting aside telephones and other devices of distraction*. You might also like to question the dominance of the restaurant or bar as default catch up venue. As the wining and dining budgets of many of our friends increased with age, your authors started suggesting alternatives to these spending-obligatory social occasions (given that a single event could easily vaporise a quarter of our weekly income). We soon noticed that the conversations we had while walking along the creek, or warming our hands round mugs of tea at a friend's kitchen table, were generally more engrossing than the distracted 'consumption-accessorised' conversations. A couple of people really can have a hell of a good time saying particular words in particular orders – BYO brain, no accessories required.

It is easy to use spending money as mental confirmation that something of value is being obtained. We can equally choose to relish and recognize value in experience, atmosphere, sensuality, or company. The more we make such choices, the less urge we have to treat ourselves by 'buying something nice' when life feels hard. That urge might become transformed into a yen to go lie in the park on a blanket and watch clouds for an hour. And before you protest that such experiential pleasures take time that most modern humans don't have, let us remind you that time is *exactly* what you can choose to have more of when you spend less money…

By the way, we're not inferring that you *shouldn't* relish your paid-for consumption – in fact it will go much further if you do. Try ordering one espresso at a café and making it last for an hour. Revel in each drop of that

---

*   Does this ring true (apologies to pun-averse readers) to you? Well there's evidence for it too. Researchers from the University of Essex put strangers into pairs to discuss 'meaningful' topics. For half of the pairs, a mobile phone was left in the room, lying discreetly on a book on a nearby desk.

Those in the room with the phone reported feeling radically less trust, empathy and overall relationship quality. It wasn't *their* mobile phone, it wasn't even switched on, and yet it affected participants' sense of connectedness even if they *didn't consciously notice the phone's existence*. One hypothesis is that a phone subconsciously suggests the possibility for alternative social connections, and thus causes us to participate less fully in the here-and-now.

oily black dynamite rolling around your taste buds. Have occasional sips of water to refresh the flavour. People-watch while you luxuriantly observe the shifts in your brain chemistry as the caffeine moves in. You'll feel astounded to witness surrounding tables fill and empty as people hurriedly consume huge meals and multiple coffees, often leaving them unfinished as they pay up and move on, seemingly unmoved by the experience. Yet simply by milking the moment for all that it's worth, you get to leave feeling like you just had a seriously decadent experience.

It might take a little practice

It is very very easy to not relish when life feels like it is thundering ever onward at such a hurly burly pace. Many people get completely out of the habit. There was a captivating passage in an otherwise rubbish book Annie read while stuck in a provincial Indonesian port town. She couldn't leave the grounds of the tiny hotel next to the airstrip for three days, because apparently once the light plane she was waiting for finally made it through a gap in the inclement weather, it would want to take off again immediately.

The book told of a pair of teenage sisters, one of whom had recently died, and was hovering as an embittered ghost over her living sibling. She was seriously resenting her non-corporeal status, and envying her sister for still having a body. In one part she watches her sister walk down a gravel driveway, and pines to feel those wet stones crunching underfoot. She swears to forgive everyone who sinned against her in life, if only some higher power will give her a mouth for just a few minutes, so that she can pick up a handful of that wet gravel and roll it around on her tongue. She imagines tasting all the different minerals, and feeling the sharp corners and the smooth facets of the gravel move against the roof of her mouth. She exults in the very thought of such sensory overload, then crashes into fury that it will never again be hers.

This passage was just perfect for a lock-in. Annie had no trouble passing the final two days in and about that little room, as she – yes – tasted gravel, investigated the sensory properties of a peanut for half an hour, and experimented with relishing the smell of the semi-rotten mangoes fallen from the tree outside her window. She also worked on her one-arm pushups.

...But is this the hand of that slightly twee cinematic heroine of relishment, Amélie, or is it the hand of your humble co-author Annie?

Some mindfulness teachers suggest starting your journey to greater sensory engagement by simply pausing whatever you're doing for five minutes, three times a day. Contemplate your surroundings and the feeling of being in your body with unhurried curiosity. Observe the contact of your feet on the ground, and the feeling of your head resting atop your spinal column. Try and sense your heart and lungs in your chest, expanding and contracting in that ceaselessly helpful way they have.

Other practitioners prescribe an exercise with a raisin, where you focus on every detail of its appearance, texture and smell for two minutes, then spend another two minutes eating it. Your authors personally prefer a cumquat. There really is *a lot* going on with a cumquat.

3. Be materialistic

'BUT WHAT?!' YOU SPLUTTER indignantly upon reading the title of this tip, 'Surely *anti*-materialism is the very cornerstone of buying less?' Upping the esteem in which you hold consumables may indeed sound an odd path to frugality, but bear with us here. Even if you're currently living a nomadic life out of a small backpack, you probably own a selection of things that help you cook, eat, bathe, sleep, work, and play. And if you'd like to avoid the constant consumption involved in replacing those things, you'll want to recognize their value, maintain them, and get things that are well-made enough in the first place that they will last and are fixable. (See also "11. Beware Fake Frugal".)

Obvious, huh? But also no longer standard modus operandi. Our culture actually seems to have become a little *averse* to looking after things: care of objects smacks of uptightness! It is unfashionable. Have you ever felt somehow uncool for reminding a friend to wipe the blades of the pruning shears you've lent them with an oily rag after use? Or coy about mentioning to your house-mate that turning the blender off before the motor begins to overheat will make it last longer?

With such an abundance of cheap things to replace broken cheap things, many of us have lost the most basic knowledge of how to care for them, and instead have almost fetishized the pleasure of not bothering. As a culture we have watched a lot of James Bond movies where the good guys blow up luxury cars and phones in the line of duty, and it seems de rigueur to not care. There is a societal suggestion that demonstrating how Fun we are involves an 'I've got more important things to do with my time' carelessness about the tawdrier aspects of material things, like looking after them. Your authors think it's a bit lame.

We are living in a material world,
so oil your bike chain regularly

Here's a suggestion. Perhaps after you've watched that James Bond movie, balance it out by watching *The Gods Must be Crazy*, which makes you feel amazed that something as beautiful and useful as a Coke bottle exists at all. Look at the slightly daggy chair at your kitchen table, and be gobsmacked by the fact that men collected sap oozing from subtropical trees to make the rubber for the nubs on its legs. Huge machines pulled the metal for its frame out of the depths of the earth and heated it until it glowed so as to extrude it into the right shape. Ancient oil was whipped into a frenzy with pigments and catalysts until it became that moulded plastic seat. Do this same thinking to the clock on your wall, the bread on your shelf, and the cheesecake in your fridge.

Be dazzled that you even have all this stuff with its stupefying lineage of effort and resources. Be reverential! Be grateful. Then look after it – the practice is sure to come back into fashion sooner or later anyway.

Forty years of blade honing – definitely a well-valued thing.

4. HAVE A LOT OF THINGS YOU WANT TO DO WITH YOUR FREEDOM

WHAT CAME FIRST, the frugality, or the egg that had a lot of things it was excited about doing? In your authors' case, definitely the excited egg. There is no better incentive for being frugal than having passions you want to chase. Let's break it down.

1. By consuming less, you have more money to spend on doing what you really want to do.

2. By consuming less, you have the option of doing less paid work, giving you more time to do what you really want to do. (Even if that happens to be chasing the kind of paid work that you really want to do.)

!. You can do a little bit of 1 and a little bit of 2 and have both the time *and* money to do the things you really want to do. Cake, and eating it.

Back when Annie was a party-hard pop-punk, she cossetted secretive visions of herself travelling through Guatemala climbing volcano after volcano, or decorating a whole house with holographic wallpaper, and knew that she'd need cash to make those things happen when the urge took her by the jugular. And so she taught herself to make the clothes she wanted out of old clothes. She made a decision to religiously love cheese and tomato sandwiches every day for lunch, while everyone around her bought takeaway kebabs. Instead of going to the pub, she cajoled friends into drinking boxed wine in deckchairs on the sidewalk (illegal but lovely) and enticed strangers into sitting down to join in. She never made a budget, or even thought about money much, but instead forged a basic assumption that most things that people spend money on have an equally satisfying cheap or free alternative. And despite her miniscule income, the savings did slowly but surely pile up. Enough that she had the freedom to go spend a couple of mind-blowingly fantastic years climbing those volcanoes.

Giving up regular untrammelled consumption actually feels quite easy when you have a sense that it is for the sake of a life studded with superior pleasures. Taking your kids on a month-long hiking trip perhaps, paying off your house, getting a weekly massage… or just taking time off work to think or do drawings.

The self-restraint of tempered consumption may seem at odds with current cultural urgings to 'live in the moment'. However, the dominant modern angle on this philosophy seems not so much Buddhist-style 'being *in* the moment', but the very impulse-spending-compatible 'living *for* the moment'. Funny that. Spontaneity is a glorious quality, but manifesting it by reliably blowing every cent you have on whatever catches your eye is not its most stellar manifestation. Putting money aside to enable life to change when you want or need it to isn't about being a financial prude. It's about not being trapped. It allows for spontaneity on a much grander scale.

If you do take up a life of spending much less and working as it suits you, you might feel as though you are doing something slightly illegal, or that 'this can't work forever. It'll come back to bite me later somehow'. Your authors know this because we were plagued by the same suspicion ourselves for many years: 'This seems like such a good a deal… surely we can't just keep getting away with it? Where's the catch?' Decades on, we have left this uncertainty in the dust. We still hardly ever think about money, we still love most of what we do most of the time, and we still appear to be very much getting away with it.

But What if I Don't Really Have Things I Want to Do?

So more freedom to choose what to do with your time is one of the fabulous side effects of spending less. Hip, hip hooray! Let's all go to the beach! Now let's watch a movie! Or maybe three movies in a row. Now let's sleep in until eleven and then spend the whole day reading *Swallows and Amazons*, eating cheese and crackers, feeling nostalgic for our lost youth, and weeping a little. Now what? What to do next when no one is making us do it? Yes, you've spotted the glitch: freedom, when we've become unaccustomed to it, can be quite daunting. If you've already had practice dealing with this, skip the rest of this tip. If you feel even a flicker of existential terror, read on.

Why does this conundrum exist at all? From a tender age society encourages us to lay aside our impetus to do things for their own sake ('intrinsic' motivation), and to instead do much of what we do for external reasons. As a young child you were almost certainly an intrinsically-motivated learner, and spent most of your waking hours *fascinated* by the world, and inventing endless adventures in pursuit of discovering how it all worked. Soon however, schooling converted learning into something you did for external motivations: grades, rewards and punishments.

Working life then continues to reinforce this pattern of doing things for external motivations. What's more, shaping your life around employment is a short cut not only to *motivation and structure,* but to social and personal *validity.* Once adapted to this set-up, people can find that as much as they might pine for holidays and crave more 'downtime', they aren't actually overflowing with ideas for what to do with this time when they get it. And fair enough. It would be a stressful existence to be constantly dreaming up things you would like to do if you don't expect to ever really have time to do them.

We'd like to make a suggestion, dear reader: if you do alter your lifestyle to give yourself more control over your own time, and then find yourself disinclined to act without external pressures, cut yourself some slack for a while. If you feel deeply decoupled from your lust for learning, and your intrinsic motivation to cha-cha with life has gone la-la, expect to even feel a little bored and lost.

Most people will need a goodly spell of recovery time using whatever extra free hours their frugal ways have scored them to both catch up on a backlog of life-maintenance activities (getting a dental check-up, cleaning out the shed) and to mooch about the house taking naps and eating peanut butter out of the jar.

At some point, you will start to feel itchy of spirit. This is the perfect time to brainstorm a list of stuff that you'd like to do. And don't you dare leave anything off that list just because it doesn't sound meaningful – most of us could come up with oodles of things we do at our jobs that are almost surrealistically meaningless, and yet we treat those as a reasonable way to spend time. If you want to spend four hours a week practising throwing circus knives, that is at least as legitimate a use of your time as spending four hours per week formatting a corporate e-newsletter to meet its style requirements, knowing all the while that no one actually cares.

The Artist as Family

One of the hallmarks of a practised Frugal Hedonist is that people are constantly asking them how they manage to take so many holidays. A Frugal Hedonist tends to work for as long as feels right, then decides to pop off to walk across Mongolia for a year. It can understandably make other people a tad peevish, as the Frugal Hedonist was likely only working part time in the first place. And probably generally seemed to enjoy their time at work – maybe because they chose their job based on what they were interested in, rather than how much money it could make them.

Let's meet a couple who no doubt elicit many perplexed questions about their unusual work/life ratio. We think their most recent adventure perfectly demonstrates how having things you're passionate about doing, can be an amazing motivation for living frugally…

Meg and Patrick have two children (Zeph, 11 and Woody, 1) and a Jack Russell terrier. The whole family (including Zero the dog)

recently spent a year travelling eastern Australia from bottom to top and back again by bicycle. Throughout the 6000 kilometre trip they sourced as much of their food as possible by foraging, hunting and barter. The journey was about having an incredible time together, but also aimed to demonstrate that a family can travel on next to no money, without relying on fossil fuels or the industrial food system. Being just as devoted as your authors are to sharing their tricks for living it up on the cheap, they've written a book about their experience – see our Further Resources section for details.

They didn't get a credit card to help pay for this trip, nor did they put in any overtime. In fact they have scarcely had time for paid work for a while now, so busy have they been producing art, a baby, a thesis, and dedicating untold hours to several community organisations in their small rural town. They can afford to be so giving with their time (and to go on adventures) because for several years their whole family's annual expenditure has been about AUD $20,000 – around one quarter of the Australian household average.

How do they do it? Giving up their cars was a pretty key step. Meg says: "Patrick saw on the RACV [the state motor vehicle association] website that it saves you $13,500 a year not having a car... we had two, so there was nearly thirty grand right there." They cook with simple whole ingredients, grow their own vegetables and eggs, and forage wild foods. They live in a non-ostentatious house and shop at second-hand shops. Their generosity with their time, energy and surplus produce within the town's community comes back to them, and they are amazed by how many of their needs end up being met by the local 'gift economy'. They describe how during the months after their son Woody was born "every time we would leave the house and come back there would be things left for us. Clothes, meals... pretty much everything a new parent could need."

Patrick says: "Life's become so much better living with the reduction of necessary income." Meg agrees: "Freedom wasn't the initial motivator," (for why they started cutting their consumption), but "it has become the main driver. For me, the more we give up, the more I want to give up."

5. HATE WASTE

AS FAR AS GREEN FURRY THINGS lurking in trash cans go, Oscar the Grouch is quite endearing in our opinion, but he isn't the only good thing you can find in a bin. Australians throw out around 20% of all food brought home – that's one grocery bag in five! Almost as much again is wasted by processors and retailers *before* it even reaches the consumer. Likewise, a staggering 40% of all food grown or imported into the US is dumped. And it's not just food we're throwing away. In the US for instance, around 150 million tonnes of unrecycled municipal waste is collected every year. Rather than come up with a visualisation based on the equivalent length of blue whales lined up end to end, can we just say this is *a freaking lot.**

Nature, which your authors are actually incredibly fond of despite mosquitoes and leeches and those hot gritty winds you get in late summer, has no concept of waste. Human societies until very recently haven't had much concept of waste. Even our grandparents' generation hardly threw away a thing – all of which shows the whole business up as rather embarrassingly unnecessary. Then came bottled water, disposable cutlery, single-portion cheese and cracker snackpacks, bread and milk so cheap that half of it is left

---

* Okay, what the hell: 150 million tonnes is the equivalent of 882,000 full size blue whales, which lined up end to end would reach around 26,000 km, two thirds of the way around the Earth!

to go mouldy, particleboard furniture, technology designed to become obsolete every year, and clothes that the culture police tell us have done the same. Our grandparents have probably turned up the Barry Manilow in heaven to block out the grunting of all those overworked garbage trucks down below.

Don't be blue gentle reader. By developing an allergy to wastefulness, you can not only diminish your role in this bizarre state of affairs, but save a surprising wallop of money too! We have personally noticed that amongst our lower-income friends, the degree to which they abhor waste is one of the biggest factors in determining whether they have any cash left at the end of the week or not.

There are three important phases to this business of becoming a non-waster. Firstly, look at **anything you're about to buy**, and assess if it has high potential to become waste*. Really badly-made anything, for instance. A new kind of moisturiser or jam 'just to try it', despite the fact that you already have plenty of moisturiser or jam. Single-use anything. Another pair of black pants in a slightly different cut from the five pairs you already have. Really deeply in-fashion anything.

You've likely heard the following advice before, but given that so many of us still forget to do it, here goes: when you're food shopping, *check what you already have before you go*. This isn't just about avoiding ending up with three jars of mayonnaise in the fridge, it's about buying stuff to complement the food you've already got. If that includes a rapidly-withering eggplant and some feta cheese that needs using, plus a few flatbreads in the freezer and rosemary in the garden, you might add garlic and tomato paste to your shopping list so you can turn it all into pizzas. If you have to buy more than you need of something, put half of it in the freezer – or knock on your neighbours' door and ask if they'd like the rest. If you only want a little of something and know you're likely to let the rest pine in the pantry, consider not getting it (!) at all.

Secondly, look at **anything you are about to throw away**, and assess its potential to be useful. If it might be valuable to someone, find somewhere to

---

*   Waste also includes overeating just to 'use something up'. Sorry.

donate it to, or put the word out on the village grapevine that it's going spare (perhaps by using one of the excellent websites that exist for advertising such things – see our Further Resources section for details). Try having a clothes swap evening with friends – they can be seriously fun, and everyone walks away with more stuff they like and less stuff they don't. Worn-out clothes can go into a rag bag and be used for cleaning or making stuff. Jars get washed and used for the kind of things jars are useful for. Older vegetables make soup; soured milk makes pancakes (the best pancakes in fact); old fruit has any bad bits cut off and is stewed.

Waste Avoidance Strategy #16

Running with our jam motif, don't throw away the jar with the final centi-metre of sticky goodness still in it – swill a little warm water around in there to loosen it up, and add it to that fruit while it's stewing. Then put it on them there pancakes. Yeah! Smidgens of leftover curry or stirfry can be added to rice with a few extra veggies and a fried egg and abracadabra! Dinner, version 2.0! Hard ends of bread can be cut into cubes, toasted and thrown into salads, soups or pasta. Where one man gazes blankly and sees nothing of value, a Frugal Hedonist sees the makings of a fine supper. See "7. Have an open relationship with recipes" for more on this.

Our third waste-busting strategy isn't for everyone, but it *will* save you the most money. **Do your shopping in the waste stream.** Your authors choose to get much of what we need from what we hereby fondly dub 'The Grand Emporium of Affluent Culture's Discarded Bounty'. If you keep your eyes peeled, and have the patience to wait for what you want, furniture, electrical equipment and building materials can generally all be scavenged from the piles people leave outside their houses, or from tip shops and junk yards. What isn't available there can often be sourced courtesy of a friend with a spare or old one that they don't use.

This strategy doesn't always result in the best quality of gear – though it can equally land you with some real gems – but it's a little like an ethical and financial Get Out of Jail Free card. If something was destined to become waste before you rescued it, you don't have to worry about the conditions under which it was made, or whether it is a 'worthy investment'. What's more, you can simply put it back out on the street if a better one comes along…

How low can you go? Do the frugal limbo!

WARNING: Several situations mentioned in the following text involve operating outside of standard supply channels. If you are going to do this, it is incredibly important to be respectful of your sources and not to wreck things for other people who might also be using them. This usually means: don't leave a mess, don't take everything for yourself, and be polite to anyone who questions what you are doing.

The shameless bird gets the worm. If you're prepared to do away with the 'But what will people think?' factor, the opportunities for meeting life's needs via stuff that would otherwise go to waste really unfold. Your authors think waste is dumb and being wily is fun, so we tend to throw pride out the window and just get in there.

We have rescued banquets of quality food from dumpsters (not to mention so many cases of beer that we've lost count). We have eaten excellent roadkill (after inspecting it for freshness and lack of disease).

We have shovelled up sacks of dried pigeon droppings from under bridges (some of the finest fertiliser to ever grace an asparagus patch). We have collected massive swags of fallen chestnuts from roadside plantings (resulting in enough of a stash in the freezer that we ate roasted chestnuts right through winter).

We have a friend who collects the compostable waste from a local organic shop, so that the shop saves on disposing of it and he gets to use it in his garden. In gratitude, they now also give him their soon-to-expire dairy products, and he gives away whatever he can't use. We have another friend who jumps in at the end of any event where all the leftover delicacies are about to be tipped into the bin, bags them up nicely, and makes sure everyone takes some home. Annie's mum tucks the paper napkins that always accompany her morning coffee into her handbag to use as tissues.

Everyone's boundaries are different, and we're not suggesting that you do things that disgust or embarrass you. But it's worth casting your eye about for unappreciated resources that you *do* feel comfortable redirecting, because it's quite a buzz to see potential where there was presumed to be none. We think of this skill as 'seeing beyond proscribed purpose', and it can mean seeing some fallen fruit as breakfast, a paper napkin as a potential tissue, or even an illness as a chance to read some good books. It's a fabulous talent to develop, because it frees you from presuming that a need can only be met by a product marketed for that purpose. Plus it certainly keeps things more interesting.

6. RECALIBRATE YOUR SENSES

WE HUMANS HAVE EMBARRASSINGLY FICKLE BRAINS. And tongues. And ears and eyes and noses. Avoid sugar for a week, and suddenly the juicy explosion of a ripe peach is transformed into the most gorgeous ambrosia your taste buds could imagine. Don't watch TV for a month, and disappearing into a book soon becomes the most captivating escapism conceivable.

'Recalibrate' is an incredibly useful word for the Frugal Hedonist, particularly because all of us have at one time or another experienced shifts in what we perceive as pleasurable. Maybe it was that time that you had a dodgy stomach and had to live on dry crackers for far too many days, then couldn't believe how good a bowl of minestrone tasted afterwards (and found yourself happily eating more simply for a while to follow...?). Maybe it was that time that the power went out for several hours, and then the lights seemed too bright and the stereo seemed too loud when they came back on (and you decided to only leave one lamp switched on for the rest of the evening...?).

The element of restriction in such scenarios undoubtedly boosts their 'reset-effect'. Adopting a consumption rhythm of lean-lavish-lean certainly intensifies pleasure. But it is not restriction that lies at the *heart* of this effect. It is contrast. And there is no reason why the activities that provide that contrast can't be enjoyable in themselves.

Think of that time you went for an amazing walk up a mountain, and the sandwich you ate when you reached the top struck you as the most satisfying thing you had ever eaten. An icy cold beer with a friend tastes about four times as good after a gratifyingly sweaty day of working in the garden together. Watching a cheesy sitcom might seem dreary if you do it all the time, but after an engrossing stint going hard at some complex mental work, it can seem like wonderful primary-coloured surrealism. Bathing regularly with hot water and soap can feel like a task as much as a luxurious experience, yet after six days of making exhilarating dashes into a chilly river while camping, that shower takes on the status of a steamy Shangri-La. Once we notice how easily such effects can occur, it only follows that we might think of exploiting them by design rather than by accident.

What a brilliant little mechanism this is! You could experiment with recalibrating what counts as a treat or outing. Pretend you're on wartime rations, and eat only the humblest of home cooking for a week – you'll want to plan your meals and maybe do an initial shop for ingredients. Then make a date to go out for ice cream during this period. That excursion is magically transformed into an enormous treat! You put on your best summer ensemble to do it, and linger over every lick, drawing the whole event out for as long as possible.

Imagine being so delicately calibrated that a cucumber could be your favourite food. *The Red Tent* by Anita Diamant is a fictionalized biography of Dinah, Jacob's only daughter in the Book of Genesis. At one point, Dinah finds herself in the heat of Egypt, far from her Mesopotamian home:

> *I was fed amazing foods … melons with orange flesh and melons with pink flesh, and there were always dates in abundance… But best of all were the cucumbers, the most delicious food I could imagine, green and sweet. Even in the heat of the sun, a cucumber kissed the tongue with the cool of the moon.*

Once your tongue has achieved cucumber-enlightenment, why not try resetting your relationship with technology? You could try a self-imposed ban on all information and entertainment technology for 48 hours (be warned, many people who do this are profoundly shocked by how much extra time the day suddenly seems to contain.) When you do open that laptop again, you might find that you are satisfied by the thrilling omniscience of just discovering what the weather will be tomorrow. Annie once made herself the guinea pig for an experiment in using no electronic technologies and no artificial light for a fortnight. She was amazed by how sensitive she became to the atmospherics of natural light by the end of it – the twinkles, glistens, sheens and glows of sunlight in its various applications became deep textural elements of each day.

We can also press reset on our expectation buttons. If you *expect* to buy takeaway for your midday meal everyday, you may be calibrated to feel that lunch is only worth looking forward to if it comes from a shop. Expect instead to always bring a packed lunch, and you'll gradually forget about the greasy displays in the shop windows, and will look forward to tucking into your roast-dinner leftovers lunchbox enormously.

Exploiting this generous agility of your body and mind is exactly what Frugal Hedonists do on a *life-long basis*. Just as the dedicated debauchee is renowned for seeking out increasingly depraved experiences to satisfy an ever more demanding appetite, frequently making frugal choices furnishes us with a more sensitive pleasure palate. The basic blueprint for modern first-world living is normalized hyper-abundance and hyper-stimulation, punctuated by desperate attempts at escape when the fallout becomes too distressing. These attempts usually take the form of bouts of restraint (like diets), or of collapse (like illness, or 'lie-by-a-pool-for-two-weeks-getting-drunk' holidays). Frugal Hedonism inverts this pattern by normalizing an elegant *sufficiency* of consumption, and then artfully dotting it with intensely relished abundance. It takes advantage of the different flavours of different modes of being, and sets them against each other to extract more enjoyment from each.

Obviously, the suggestions we've made so far are for quite small-fry recalibrations (although you may be surprised by the ripple effects.) If you're hungry for something grander, why not try recalibrating your fundamental concept of 'middle'? You could kick off with a little learning binge about people who deliberately live at extremes of the low-spending spectrum, such as those who

Everything's amazing. Nobody's happy.

"Everybody on every plane should just constantly be going 'Oh my God, wow!' You're flying. You're … you're sitting in a chair in the sky! But 'It doesn't go back a lot'. And 'It smells really'. You know, here's the thing: people say there's delays on flights. Delays. Really? New York to California in five hours. That used to take thirty years to do that, and a bunch of you would die on the way there, and have a baby. You'd be with a whole different group of people by the time you got there. Now you watch a movie, you take a dump, and you're home."

~ Louis C. K.

One of your authors was on a plane recently where a few passengers *were* very excited about being on a chair in the sky – they were children. When they first started yelling "We're going off the grouuuuund! We're really flyyyyying! We're going inside a clouuud!!!!" other passengers shifted about their seats, unsure whether to be irritated or not. Then they started smiling and craning their necks to look out the windows a little, and felt briefly delighted and flabbergasted by the whole situation.

travel without money, or eat 'freegan'* style. Perhaps watch some documentaries that look at the lifestyles and resource-use expectations of your average modern shanty-town dweller. Delve into the lives of some icons of history, whose definitions of convenience and comfort were inevitably more forgiving than those of their modern counterparts (see "10. Romanticise other eras" for more on this). Look at some of the stuff that kids get excited about, and question whether your capacity for noticing the 'impressive' in things has become blinkered with age. Making these kind of mental forays now and again can be an invigorating reality check, and a refreshing counterbalance to whatever exposure you're getting to jaded middle class lifestyle standards.

Truly hardwiring your frugal recalibration doesn't happen overnight. Sure, your body is spectacularly nimble in its adaptability. Your mouth only needs a few days off from additive-inflated fast food flavours to find a tomato and basil salad lip-smackingly delectable. Your muscles grow strong and tenacious enough to dig in a garden for hours after only a few weeks of practice. But you will likely find that your mental habituation to specific behaviours and expectations is a little more stubborn. (See also "13. Listen to the habit scientists…".) Be patient, and gloat over every little increase in your capacity for pleasure that your recalibrations score for you along the way. Embrace the spirit of self-experimentation! Don't stop until you can wax lyrical about a cucumber!

---

*   Freegan: a person who bases their diet around utilising otherwise unvalued food, usually motivated by a desire to reduce environmental impact. This may include rescuing superficially damaged food from dumpsters, harvesting from ignored fruit trees, wild foraging, and passing surplus produce around between friends.

7. HAVE AN OPEN RELATIONSHIP WITH RECIPES

YOU ENCOUNTER THE CONCEPT of the latest famous chef's pinenut-studded hotcakes with caramelised quince compote, and feel a sudden passion to possess it, just like The One In The Picture. It may almost feel important – as if your life would be a better life with that dish in it, a meal that someone has bothered to write about and place in a shaft of sunlight on a scrubbed wooden table to photograph. It probably is quite yummy too. But be warned, dear reader! Make a frequent habit of faithful recipe replication, and you will spend oodles on one-off ingredients, many of which will have exactly two and a half teaspoons removed from the jar, before swiftly segueing from Essential to... mouldering in the back of the fridge.

The Frugal Hedonist chooses a culinary path of more flair and independence. Develop some cooking instincts and then base your meals on whatever happens to be in season, cheap, or in the cupboard right now. Go totally freestyle, or if you do like to use recipes, learn to substitute. No breadcrumbs to help bind your meatballs? Grind some oats in a blender and use those instead. No apple cider vinegar, but plenty of lemons? Lemon juice plus a pinch of sugar will probably be just fine. Most deliciousness is a push and pull between sweet, sour, and salty elements, with a tasty fat to carry the flavour (and to help you absorb the nutrients). Also consider including something with bitter notes to cut richness, or an *umami* component to give robust savouriness, and things will usually turn out scrumptiously. If all that fails, grill some extra cheese on the top.

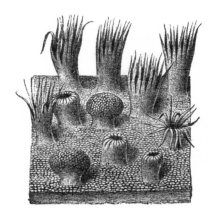

Your taste buds as imagined by Gray's Anatomy (1918).
They certainly look ready to party.

This is how all the fancy stuff gets invented anyway! Italian peasant Z did not decide to squeeze the juice of unripe grapes onto meat so that it could later be marketed in small bottles as verjuice and make lots of dosh for gourmet food companies. Peasant Z did it because they recognized that their dinner would taste better with a sour note, and had nothing else acidic on hand. Your authors find that our own cuisine escalates in sublimeness the more we come to rely on the random. A harvest of chestnuts and under-ripe apples lead to a fabulous goat, chestnut, and tart apple stew. A yen for Earl Grey tea provokes experiments with steeping a sprig of thyme in regular tea, which turns out to be super nice.

We do use recipes for learning. A good trick is to find three recipes for something similar to what you want to make. Then see where they overlap to give you a rough idea of proportions. For example, we had lots of nettles and potatoes in the garden, and some haloumi that needed using, so we looked up a few gnocchi recipes to get a feel for ratios and essential preparation techniques. (If we hadn't already had the flour called for by all three gnocchi recipes, we would have just made a fry-up with our ingredients instead.) Recipes are also good for trying out whole new flavour combinations that use the raw ingredients you find yourself with in even more artful ways – green tomato pie anyone? But, basically, in the words attributed to Charlie Parker,

"Master your instrument, master the music, and then forget all that shit and just play." You'll know you've gotten there when you have friends coming for dinner and you make a gravy that involves Vegemite, with complete confidence that no one will notice.

Vegemite Gravy
(you can use Marmite or Promite if you are from a Non-Vegemite-Worshipping-Nation)

Okay, we recognize the irony of including a recipe here, but what the heck…

> Butter (or lard, or ghee, or oil)
>
> Onion, very finely chopped (optional, but it's nice to add some garlic or mushrooms at the end of step 5 if you don't use it)
>
> Plain flour (if using cornflour instead, use much less and mix to a smooth paste with a little water before putting into the pan with the fat)
>
> Stock made from bones/meat/vegetable scraps, or water and half a stock cube… or just use plain water
>
> Vegemite (or a glug of soy sauce)
>
> Some old red wine (or red wine vinegar)
>
> Rosemary or thyme or both, finely chopped
>
> Salt and pepper

1. Melt knob of butter in a frypan over medium heat, and fry onions gently until really soft, then remove them from the pan.

2. Melt a small knob of butter in pan, then remove from heat.

3. Slowly mix a spoonful of flour into the butter to make a paste (a roux).

4. Return pan to a low heat and quickly start stirring in some stock until you have something with a consistency like cream.

5. Add about a teaspoon of Vegemite, a dash of wine, the rosemary and some salt and pepper.

6. Cook while stirring for about 5 minutes, or until thick and tasty.

8. Don't be a sucker

Over half a trillion dollars is spent globally each year on PR and advertising. If you live in the US, UK or Australia, around $US1000 (in 2013 terms) is spent on you personally. We'd love to save the advertisers all that needless bother, since we don't think much of it works on us, and simply accept a cheque. Or the equivalent value in whisky.

And while talking-up your product is far from a new phenomenon, not only have 'persuasion specialists' now had decades to refine their nefarious arts, but the sums currently being put at their disposal are a whole new kind of astronomical. In Germany for example, spending on online advertising alone is seven times the entire budget of the Nazi propaganda machine at its peak (adjusting for inflation). And few of us would deny the power *that* expenditure had to persuade people into a rotten value system.

Advertisers know that appealing to your rational side – merely promoting a product's tangible attributes – is not very effective. Far more powerful is to suggest, whether blatantly or surreptitiously, that you don't have everything that you deserve, or everything that you *should* have in order to be acceptable. They romance you by implying that there is a sort of life that is Right For You Personally, and that they have the stuff to sell that goes with that life. Homewares that have a whiff of sturdy farmhouse simplicity (because that more honest way of life really resonates with you), super cute socks (because you're a playful girlish type of woman), huge plasma screen TVs (because you take entertainment seriously), or expensive Catalan beers (because you appreciate that European dedication to quality produce and regional specialties). Complex psychology is used to ensure that the marketing plays to your most precious visions of the You you'd like to be, and the What you feel like life should be more like. Who could blame a body for falling prey to a seduction aimed so meticulously at that vulnerable underbelly of dreams and insecurities…?

Increasingly, even those of us who like to think ourselves savvy to such tricks are being catered to by advertisers! Witness the evolution of products, shops, cafés and magazines whose branding is designed to suggest a get-away-from-the-hype aesthetic, loveable by discerning people who aren't into commercialism and all that rubbish. Witness the recent genre that is the 'self-aware' ad. This generally pokes fun at the cheap tricks of advertising, and then implies itself to be in a different and more honest category. Or it may hilariously confess outright that it is trying to suck you in - somehow making you feel like it's okay when you succumb. Laughs all round.

So what to do? One of your rather stubborn authors has been known to mutter under her breath "You won't get me that easily, you crafty devil!" when becoming aware that her gaze is lingering on the perfectly-pitched font of some gourmet packaging, but we realise that won't work for everyone. Never fear, there are some other tricks you can keep up your sleeves…

Do the maths. Totally invert one of the most basic strategies of advertising by practising this simple habit: when you see a lot of ads for something, consider that a large chunk of the price of that product is paying for those ads, rather than for product quality or value. By this logic, the more it is advertised, the more overpriced it is.

Be more content. Okay, easier said than done, but as author Douglas Rushkoff writes in his book *Coercion*, "the more fun you're having in life, the more satisfied you are with yourself, the harder a target you are to reach." You may have observed that people with an air of contentment with life, a mind fascinated by ideas, and strong connections with other people and the natural world are less susceptible to advertising. So make like a content person, and ignore the billboard! You are above such piffle!

Deep truth in advertising

The ancient Greek philosopher Epicurus taught that three things are essential for a happy life: friendship, freedom, and time for contemplation. Alain de Botton (a much more modern philosopher) has noted that advertisers frequently associate their product with one of these three ingredients, slyly tapping into what people *actually* feel that their lives need more of.

For more on Epicurus and his most frugal brand of hedonism, see our box in "30. People who need people…".

The advertising executive who commissioned this one must have been feeling nervous and insisted that all three of Epicurus' principles of happiness be squeezed in: freedom, friendship and contemplation.

Just see fewer ads. Stop watching TV, at least in any form that includes commercials. People with small children manage to do this too, we promise. Wherever possible, shop at small stores and markets instead of megamalls and supermarkets. The latter options put you at the mercy of a 360° environment designed specifically to encourage you to buy. If you do need to go to one of these places, try treating the displays and sales posters as inconsequential wallpaper. Do the same with billboards, and if you buy newspapers, remove any catalogues and put them straight in the recycling. Finally, we seriously suggest avoiding any kind of lifestyle magazine or liftout like the pox. More on why this is so helpful is conveniently located in our very next tip.

9. STOP READING THOSE MAGAZINES

SURELY, THIS IS THE LIFE! Flipping through the easily digestible pages of lifestyle media while ingesting something with hollandaise sauce on it on a Sunday morning. Sometimes you detect a trickle of adrenaline phwoof into your bloodstream as you scan the pages full of appealing things you could be having and doing... but probably won't.

The language in the columns you're skimming cosies up to you, making you feel as if these people that write this stuff, do this stuff, have this stuff and live this life are Your People; that you 'get' each other. It only follows that you should measure yourself by the bars they seem to be setting. That it makes sense for you to throw about phrases like 'time-poor' and 'retail therapy', because *they* do.

Problem is, They are not you. In fact They are mostly not even Them, but just writers attempting to satisfy an expected tone, spitting out blurbs about a Ethiopian fusion restaurant with award-winning décor, or a great new line of handbags in the shape of marine mammals. Meanwhile, they muddle on with their imperfect lives, eat pasta, and go to the shops carrying an old tote with a frayed strap, just like we all do.

Very few people actually do much of the stuff that the media implies people do, and those who do work hard to keep up. But lifestyle journalism makes it easy to feel that there is a world of people out there effortlessly dressing, holidaying, exercising, eating and thinking in certain appropriate ways, and it is in human nature to not want to be terribly out of line with what everyone else is up to. Steer clear of this homogenising influence is your authors' suggestion. Spend your Sunday morning breakfasts perusing odd facts about breeding piranhas in captivity instead.

Sample facial expressions you might like to experiment with while declining to read lifestyle magazines. Second from the right is a pet leopard, Julian, who takes no interest at all in media culture.

10. ROMANTICISE OTHER ERAS

NO MATTER HOW CONFIDENTLY you stride through the world, leaving a mangled trail of snubbed advertising in your wake, a bit will still get stuck to your socks here and there. Escaping seduction by advertising's lifestyle-romanticising is ultimately impossible to do using strength of will alone. And you certainly wouldn't want to do it by rejecting romance.

Most ads carry a subliminal message that we all have the power of self-creation, and that what they are selling can help us with that. This can only be countered by replacing their suggested romantic visions of ourselves with *other romantic visions*. You might even like to call it self-administered advertising.

Where can we find these other visions? Looking to the world around you for people that you find inspiring in terms of strength, contentment and panache is a great start. But why not really cast your net wide? Look at history. Look at fiction. Look at other animals if that's what best gets you romanticising how Jaunty-Free-And-Drinking-Only-Ice-Melt-Water-To-Quench-Your-Thirst you'd secretly like to be.

While both your authors can lay claim to some impressive childhood nerd credentials, it is Annie who was (and still is) a certifiable library nerd. So we'll let her rhapsodise on the mental moulding power of the novel a while:

> I remember first reading about Ernest Shackleton's Antarctic journeys as a young teenager. I was fascinated and intoxicated by how the

exploration team compensated for their meagre rations and harsh travelling conditions by becoming more spirited and inventive. Then I came across *Tracks*, Robin Davidson's account of her solo journey by camel across the arid interior of Australia in the 1970s. Then *Robinson Crusoe*, which could kindle a desire to craft a bowl out of a coconut in even the most Gucci-clad bosom. At the same time I was lapping-up whodunnits featuring a canny medieval peasant lass as sleuth, and working my way through John Steinbeck's dustbowl-era classics.

I recently re-read Roald Dahl's *Matilda*. Matilda is a genius child born into a cruel, rich, idiotic family who don't appreciate her talents. Miss Honey, Matilda's kindly school teacher, does however, and in one scene Matilda visits Miss Honey's home. In the kitchen, there are no taps over the sink, and a shelf and a single cupboard are the only furniture. On the shelf is a Primus stove, and a saucepan. Miss Honey sends Matilda to the well for water, then asks:

"I don't suppose you've ever done that before?"

"Never," Matilda said. "It's fun. How do you get enough water for your bath?"

"I don't take a bath," Miss Honey said. "I wash standing up. I get a bucketful of water and I heat it on this little stove and I strip and wash myself all over."

"Do you honestly do that?" Matilda asked.

"Of course I do," Miss Honey said. "Every poor person in England used to wash that way until not so very long ago. And they didn't have a Primus. They had to heat the water over the fire in the hearth."

"Are you poor, Miss Honey?"

"Yes," Miss Honey said. "Very. It's a good little stove isn't it?" The Primus was roaring away with a powerful blue flame and already the water in the saucepan was beginning to bubble. Miss Honey got a teapot from the cupboard and put some tea leaves into it. She also found half a small loaf of brown bread. She cut two thin slices...

Although this scene exists to describe the poverty of Miss Honey, it kindled in me a perverse envy for the intense simplicity of her domestic life. I have had periods of my life where I have had to heat water to bathe. I haven't forgotten that there are some days where you pine for the convenience of a hot shower, but overall, the pared-back quality of those times is associated with happiness for me. And the way that simple things swell in value when there is 'less' is inherent in this passage: the wonder at the Primus' efficiency, the savouring of the bread and tea we can project will happen because of their preciousness.

My love affair with literary portrayals of spirit and sass in a context of material scarcity has never abated. It is not the scarcity itself that matters, but rather the message that spunkiness, good friendships, and an amazing life are not dependent on buying stuff. All this romanticising – 'advertising' – to myself of these possibilities has certainly been partially responsible for some of my life direction since. Specifically, long distance hiking, hitchhiking and other travelling with very minimal funds and gear. More generally, a pleasure in thrift and resourcefulness, and an ongoing preference for experiences over possessions, and freedom over status.

MANY OF US TELL ADMIRING, nostalgia-drenched tales about the resourcefulness and spirit of our grandparents in the face of harder times. We marvel at how war-time rationing improved people's health and forged strong communities as neighbours came to rely more on each other than on purchasing power for both necessities and recreation. We speak with a twinkle of envy about the simplicity of life in 'the olden days', or the unencumbered freedom of cattle-drovers and swagmen. We digest the stories of long sea voyages to strange shores, or of forging a life in a new land, and we quietly ache to put our own tenacity to the test in such a way, if only a little.

Partly these undercurrents of emotion come from a basic human appreciation for strength. Partly they speak of a yen to feel that we are living 'real lives', challenged to capacity. Perhaps even that part of us which has noticed how food is tastier, rest is sweeter, and love is more vivid when we aren't so swaddled in cottonwool, craves a little more deprivation for the sake of these stronger joys that come with it.

Our ideas about what constitutes value and success shift almost eagerly in response to stories of such lives. It is then up to each of us how much we heed *these* ideas instead of those brought on by the plump polish of advertising culture, and also how much we feed ourselves more such stories.

Check out the list of potential frugally-romantic fodder in our Further Resources section.

Bar of Frugal Legends: Robinson Crusoe, Epicurus, Ernest Shackleton and Miss Honey. Now, who's buying the first round?

11. BEWARE FAKE FRUGAL

LISTEN UP, THIS IS QUITE an important bit. Maybe it should have gone right up the front. Right next to the definition of frugality. Because this is actually a sub-clause of that very definition: if it is cheap to buy, but at the expense of someone or something else, it's Fake Frugal, and it's just not fair. Factory-farmed eggs, endless brand new clothes made by tired women in far away countries, 'value packs' of disposable razors that end up as bobbing carpets in the North Atlantic. You get the gist.

Buying cheap disposable, or crummy quality things that quickly need replacing, is not only Fake Frugal because it leads to you spending more money later on, but because it leads to us all living in a very non-hedonism-compatible rubbish dump. An example might be those can openers that only cost $2.99 but aren't actually can openers, just something kind of *shaped* like a can opener. Or all that furniture which looks flash in the store, but sags as soon as damp weather comes along. When part of it pops off because somebody looks at it too hard, you can't even nail it back on, because the particleboard takes on the structural integrity of branflakes after three weeks out of the factory. You get all irritated and wan-feeling about the shoddiness of things, stick it in a dark corner of the garage hoping it will magically disappear, and go out shopping for another cupboard.

This equation applies to health too. If the el cheapo bread you eat as a staple is so stripped of nutrients that you end up with a depressed immune system, leading to more sick days and being forced to down pricey supplements, it's not really cheap bread any more is it?

The price tags on foods that are produced conscientiously might seem steep compared to those of industrial foods. But consider this: modern first world citizens spend a teensy percentage of our incomes on stocking our pantries compared to any other culture in the history of time, and we still seem to think it costs us too much!* When in a store deciding what to buy, most of us compare prices between competing products. And if the organic yoghurt is a couple of dollars more, that can feel too expensive. Yet this is generally a warped lens to scrutinise those couple of dollars through, given that most of us wouldn't notice that amount of money when compared to the sums we spend on a muffin and coffee later on in the day, at the bottleshop on the way home, or going online to buy phone credit or a concert or plane ticket that night. Your authors did fluff around over buying organic nuts for a while, because the price difference seemed astronomical. But once we thought about it, it still struck us as a fair price for a nut well-grown, so we made the switch. Now we just eat fewer nuts, and they seem more exquisite.

Folks of yore barely wasted a scrap of food because they handed over respectable sums of money for it. These higher prices reflected the true 'costs' of producing food much more accurately: back when farms were all small and organic, farmers had to preserve the health of their soil and water using methods that could be sustained by the local area if they wished to keep on farming there; they passed on these ecosystem maintenance costs along with the other costs of production. For the last few decades, large scale industrialized farming has increasingly been deferring these costs (such as loss of top soil, carbon emissions and fertilizer pollution) to be dealt with by poorer peoples and future generations. If we stop wasting money on wasting food and spend it on giving farmers a better sum for their wares, it means they aren't stuck using damaging systems just to be able to make a living.

When a merchant banker pays $300,000 for a beat-up old piece of sports or music memorabilia, it's because there is a story embedded in that object that they like thinking about. Similarly, when we buy goods produced with real care and big-picture intelligence, they come with a backstory rich with positive feedback loops that feel pretty damn good to think about, which

---

* This disparity exists even when comparing fairly recent decades: the percentage of their incomes that Americans spend on food has *halved* since the 1950s.

makes their purchase seem like a bigger, more satisfying experience. By extension, if you buy things that rely on continued destruction or suffering for their production, you're paying for a depressing backstory, which you'll probably end up blocking out any awareness of… leaving you with *no* story, and a product that feels rather one-dimensional. You are also forced to create dark taboo corners in your mind, which are surely a hindrance to gloriously expansive feelings of wonder and connectivity. That's quite a sacrifice to make!

In a nutshell? We foolish humans cheat ourselves when we try to save money by buying crap stuff that requires us to spend more money replacing it, or leads to us living with crap health on a crap planet – since what we were trying to do in the first place was spend less money and have a good life. Holistic thinking and all that. Let's get stuck into it.

Sustainable supping on a shoestring

Want to dine in good conscience, but haven't got much dough to do it? Fret no longer! By focussing your sustainable dollar on high-value foods (and tweaking your meals to use these foods more), you can still end up with a high proportion of what you eat coming from ethical sources.

For example, your authors have sussed-out that in our area organic carrots, potatoes, onions, turnips, beets and pumpkin come pretty cheap year-round. Work out what your local equivalents are – if you get to answer "organic mangoes and custard apples are generally very cheap where I live", we officially hate you. Staple grains, legumes, and tinned tomatoes are also mostly very affordable even when organic, as are seeds (sesame, chia, sunflower, flax). Keeping your eye firmly on that price-per-kilo, compile a list of other random affordable things that you could make good use of.

Organic milk is still an excellent value foodstuff, despite being much pricier than its non-organic counterpart. The same goes for organic stock bones and beef liver, which your authors use to make incredibly tasty and nutritious broth and pâté respectively. As Australians, we also have access to affordable kangaroo meat – the mince is the cheapest so we buy that the most, and turn it into Bolognese, patties, and so on. The most sustainable fish are the little oily ones like sardines and mackerel, which also happen to be some of the cheapest and healthiest!

If you take the above food list, and add homegrown and foraged greens, herbs, and fruit (which conveniently, are three of the easiest things to grow and forage), you've got a lot of your bases covered. Even if you're still buying the other thirty per cent of your groceries from non-organic sources, you're doing pretty darn well. Top it off by paring back your consumption of processed and packaged foods, and you're headed towards a diet so delicious, healthy, and cheap that it will be the envy of chefs, nutritionists, and accountants alike…

Some truly frugal meals from your authors' table: (L) porridge made from organic oats, with homegrown bottled apricots, foraged blackberries, organic sultanas, non-organic cream and cinnamon, plus pistachio nuts rescued from a dumpster (total cost per serve: 60c); (R) broth made from organic beef bones, with mixed foraged wild greens and lemon juice, organic carrots and swedes, non-organic rice noodles and spices, eggs from a friend's chicken, homegrown coriander and spring onions ($1.95 per serve)

12. Enjoy excess

WE HAVE VIRTUALLY NO EVIDENCE to support our claims here, but your authors suspect it's mighty unwholesome to live by *any* ethos 365 days a year. Your neural pathways need regular shake-ups to keep them nice and elastic, so we advocate periodic abandonment of all forms of regular behaviour.

There is a risk for some frugalists of becoming fixated on only consuming the necessary minimums, or only doing what is functional. This may be frugality, but it is *not* Frugal Hedonism. The Frugal Hedonist regularly prioritises and indulges in the unnecessary! Frolicking in the ocean for hours, making leisurely love, falling asleep in the park all afternoon, or staying up until dawn to finish a gripping book. This kind of abandon is, if anything, *more* available to the person who is not burying themselves in a stupor of fiscally-supplied indulgences. Your authors suggest using the extra free time and inventiveness you acquire as a Frugal Hedonist to be behaviourally excessive and frivolous as often as desired. Here are some sample possibilities:

~ Devote an entire late summer's day to wandering the streets and alleyways of your neighbourhood sampling overhanging fruit.

~ Get up in pre-dawn blackness on a morning when you don't have to, set yourself up somewhere reverential, and watch the sun come up.

~ Eat spaghetti bolognese with your fingers… or without using your hands at all.

~ Listen to opera at maximum volume, in the bath, in the dark. Or maybe that kind of death metal that sounds strangely similar to opera.

There is however, also a special place in Frugal Hedonism for really abandoning yourself to excessive *consumption* now and again. Firstly, we think it satiates a very basic human urge to blow material moderation to Timbuktu once in a while. Secondly, it is beautifully protective against twinges of jealousy that may rear up as you watch the consumer society around you incessantly gorging itself – when you get to throw limits to the wind now and again, but suffer none of the damage that comes with *ongoing* over-consumption, you truly do feel like you're getting the best of both worlds.
One of your authors likes to satisfy this need with an occasional session of staying up into the small hours and watching English murder mysteries while dunking chocolate biscuits in whisky. There are classier options available, of course. A friend of ours has an oyster farmer in the family, and sometimes brings home a whole sackload of the ones that are under commercial weight, dishing them out to guests sprawled on a blanket in her garden until no one can eat another oyster.

An excess of a single ingredient actually seems to make excess feel even more excessive, and this factor makes seasonal gluts a perfect starting point for consumption bonanzas. We hosted a banana party when our palms last produced way more than we could ever eat by ourselves. We dragged half the pot plants in the garden inside to make a jungle, stuck up some monkey pictures, and requested that our guests wear yellow and bring something that could be combined with bananas. We ended up with flambés, daiquiris, and banana-peanut-butter jaffles being eaten to Hawaiian music, as people shared odd banana trivia and waxed surprisingly lyrical over their personal relationships with the yellow curvy fruit.

Mass cultural events of material excess can also be good. Think Halloween trick-or-treating, and Easter egg hunts – the latter at least being as available to adults as to children. Just don't fall prey to engaging in holiday-themed shopping for the whole month leading up to the occasion, as retailers now encourage so unabashedly. After all, pulses of excessive consumption only become valuable if your life is otherwise one of material leanness. In *this* context, they offer the intoxication of breaking all the rules, and acquire their proper glory. They can also make us feel quite relieved about a return to regular life… once the stomach ache wears off.

Ready, aim, gazpacho!

La Tomatina, the annual tomato-throwing festival in the Valencian town of Buñol, is the world's largest food fight, with an estimated 150,000 tomatoes being hurled into a pulp throughout the day. This frenzy of profligacy is hardly an extension of a year-round culture of excess. It actually occurs in a region where the inhabitants have little choice but to be frugal with resources in their daily lives (the average income per capita in the region, even adjusted for purchasing power, is around half that of the United States).

The festivities take place on the last Wednesday in summer, kicking off with the *palo jamón*: a game in which revellers attempt to topple a ham off a tall greasy pole, while the crowd cheers and dances. With the touching of the ham, trucks carrying the tomatoes enter the square, and the fight begins. After an hour of impassioned tomato tossing, the streets are a red river. Water hoses signal the end of the fight, and the thickly coated celebrators are washed down.

Most traditional cultures have feast days and other frenzies of material excess incorporated into their calendar. Perhaps they understood the value of devoting some resources to occasions of extravagance, to invert the material conservatism that has been the necessary mode of day-to-day life for most of human history. Possibly our psychological craving for such events goes right back to the influxes of super-abundant meat that would have followed a large game kill in hunter-gatherer societies. Groups who still live this way have been noted to engage in marathon dance sessions on the day a kill is brought home.

We're pretty sure that partying has so often gone with abundance partly because it's nice to have a full belly, but there is a possible further function of the feast-fiesta. Making your occasions of profligate consumption into a good hoo-ha, or a conscious ritual, highlights them in your memory, where they act as strong confirmation to your psyche that you have 'enough' (just as giving does – see "49. Give something"). It often seems that the rampant consumption that characterises modern affluent culture is a response to a feeling of never quite having 'enough'. So ironically, peppering your life with punctuation marks of emphatic excess may be an excellent defence against hankering after every sugary or shiny commodity that prances your way.

13. Listen to the Habit Scientists. Yes, they have those now.

We humans are creatures of habit, and a very adaptive trait it is too. Mental processes burn up a heck of a lot of (historically) precious kilojoules, so evolution has designed us to favour even flawed automatic behaviours over repeatedly using time and energy to think about what would be good to do in every individual situation.*

Giving these entrenched behaviours a makeover isn't always easy. As if the sound of your evolutionary brain yelling at you for wasting kilojoules whenever you try to change a teeny tiny habit wasn't offputting enough, consider this: although self-discipline is now talked about as though it were a fundamental personality component, it hasn't been much of a player until the last few centuries of our evolution. When your basic daily activities are absolutely necessary to provide you with food and shelter for the immediate future, there is unlikely to be any faffing along the lines of 'Oh, golly, can I *really* be

---

* What's more, if we unquestioningly adopt an entire cultural *template* of behaviours, we can save even the initial brain-energy that we'd need to create habits we actually *want*. No wonder we feel compelled to just 'go with the flow'!

bothered going foraging today?' Also no need to manifest the discipline to CONSTANTLY NOT EAT CHOCOLATE CAKE, or to not play World of Warcraft for nineteen hours straight. We are surrounded by a kaleidoscopic wealth of tantalizing hyper-stimulation and easy calories, but we haven't had a long time to get very good at this discipline thing.

The happy news is that research has indicated that willpower functions like a muscle, and the more you exercise it, the stronger it gets. As with other muscles, your progression to Schwarzeneggeresque will go better if you start off with stuff you can handle, and build up gradually. And willpower trumps big biceps (Arnold may disagree with this) in terms of life knock-on effects: studies have shown that people who consciously flex some willpower in one area – sticking to an exercise plan for example – tend to automatically use it more in other aspects of their lives – not overspending perhaps.*

However, habit scientists suggest that relying solely on willpower to change ingrained habits is fallible. If you're rundown or unwell your willpower muscle loses oomph, just as your physical ones do. The trick, apparently, is to not even attempt using sheer force of will to resist behaviours that you want to change. Instead, *notice* the urge, and then put a different behaviour there in response to it.

"You know, I think I *will* take a packed lunch tomorrow"

Perhaps when you have a crummy day at your job, your urge for pleasure and escapism leads to spending big on beer and pizza and watching inane TV all evening. If you'd like to change this habit, try acknowledging the

---

* One clause here: just as you probably wouldn't pump iron like never before AND enter an arm wrestling tournament on the same day, really flexing your willpower muscle in any given area depletes your daily allowance of it, even though you're building your willpower fitness in the long term. So if you've sworn you'll finish your tax return before dinner tonight, don't plan on skipping dessert too, because you might not have enough discipline for number crunching and dietary restraint all at once.

Seize the day

Habits are dogged things, whereas the rush of motivation that comes with epiphany is fleeting, no matter how vivid it may feel at the time. So if you are ever feeling inspired to revamp some aspect of your life (perhaps, dare we be so presumptuous, by something within these very pages…?), you likely have but a wee window of opportunity to convert inspiration into action.

You might begin by jotting down a few specific, realistic changes you'd like to turn into habits, or bits of your life that you think could be rejigged. Starting with realisable goals means you can witness the success and effects of your choices pretty quickly, leading to positive reinforcement and a heady sense of mastery over your own behaviour! These pleasant feelings can kickstart a shift in direction that has its own momentum.

Or you could dive straight in! Insert instant Frugal Hedonism by deciding not to go to that café for breakfast this morning; go for a decadently long stroll instead, and pick up enough good eggs and cream to make deluxe omelettes for a whole week of breakfasts. You've already saved twenty bucks, gotten some exercise, and had a dandy morning.

If you're feeling bolder, set the ball rolling on something grander. Something that sabotages the chance of relapse. Give yourself one week to calculate whether you could manage without… ooh, your car, for example… If you decide by the end of that time that you can tweak all the vital elements enough to make it work, sell the thing. Big or small changes – run with your personal style here. The important thing is to do them *soon*, while you're still riding that fizzy crest of the wave of insight…

urge and what cued it, but then invent a response that satisfies that urge in a way that you feel better about. Perhaps eating soup and buttery toast while re-reading a favourite book in bed all evening. Or putting punk rock on your headphones and going for a frenzied walk to a hill you like to watch the sunset from. Invent these substitutions in times when you're feeling potent and inspired, and once you've experienced a pleasure rush from them enough times, they become new habits, and you'll go to them gladly even when you're feeling wilted-of-will.

Another fantastic strategy for taking some of the load of habit change off your willpower muscle is to make a few blanket decisions, thereby neatly sidestepping hundreds of small willpower-sapping ones - see "39. Limit the burden of choice" for more on this.

14. DON'T BUY DRINKS

WE DON'T MEAN NEVER, but we do mean *almost* Never. In general, those drink bastards charge you mostly for the bottle and branding, or for the service if you're in a café or restaurant. If the tap water in your area is safe to drink, bottled water is absurd (and not only from a financial point of view), and fizzy drinks and most juices are basically sugar. They frequently cost nearly half as much as your meal, and add relatively nutritionless calories while they're at it.

Keep a bottle of water in your bag instead, and refill it from the nearest tap when it's low. If you're having a sit-down meal, don't just automatically find something on the menu because the waitperson says "... and to drink?" Order a drink only if you really want one, and ask for a glass of water otherwise. People are often shocked by how much money they can save this way, and with little sense of suffering.

Exceptions we personally like to make are for ritualistic drinks that stand in place of eating out. Perhaps a random vino at an outdoor table as the sun goes down, the buying of which gives you license to sit and watch the passing crowds for a while.

As for alcohol more generally, drinking at home (or on a friend's porch, or on a picnic blanket placed in a suitably salubrious location) is obviously cheaper, especially if you enjoy brewing your own. If we plan on having a couple of drinks, your authors tend to shun pubs or bars in favour of these more 'teenage' locations – it was fun then, and it's fun now! We also highly recommend getting a second-hand fur scarf or something, so you can feel luxurious while drinking cheap gin.

	FOOD	*DRINK*
VERY CLASSY RESTAURANT	Main $54	Cheapest glass of wine $23
CLASSY RESTAURANT	Main $26	Cheapest glass of wine $9
HIP CAFÉ	Lunch $17.50	Fresh juice $6.50
VIETNAMESE SOUP BAR	Large soup $9.80	Juice $3.50
CONVENIENCE STORE	Sandwich $5	Medium soft drink $4.40
FAST FOOD RESTAURANT	Hamburger $4.80	Medium soft drink $2.75

Actual sample prices from some venues around Melbourne, Australia. We rest our case!

What comes next is pretty cheeky. Your cunning authors are about to sneak a *whole extra frugal strategy* in under the 'Don't buy drinks' heading. It is actually one of the top money-saving strategies in this entire book, but we suspected some of you might avoid reading it if it announced itself: if you really want to spend less, eat out less.

Current generations are eating out *way* more than previous ones, laying out serious money for the privilege (and contributing to current weight and food-waste crises via the ingredient profile and size of meals prepared away from home). If you're a dab hand in the kitchen, cooking at home in a creative cloud of steam and spices produces dishes at least as tasty as what you get when you go out, and for a tenth of the price. Eating out less also makes it into much more of a treat when you *do* do it. Find a couple of cheap places that you really like, so that you get maximum bang for your dining buck – like a noodle bar that churns them out hot and fresh and has a two-for-one deal on Monday nights that you can make an occasion out of now and again.

We've already sung the praises of the packed lunch, so we won't go there again now, but don't forget the packed snack! If you know you're going to be out and about for a long stretch, stuff some hardy food items like an apple and a few nuts into your bag so you're not forced to blow cash on tiny tubs of overpriced sugary yoghurt from convenience stores. The essential attitude change inherent in all the above suggestions is that food, by default, comes from home, and getting it from elsewhere is a deliberate indulgence, not just what happens whenever you need to eat. The savings resulting from this mental shift can be huge. Which can directly contribute to you working less, and having time for more experiences that don't involve trawling Urbanspoon for hours…

Pollution issues aside, imagine you're stranded on a desert island. Who will ever find your message in a bottle?

15. FIND FREE 'THIRD' PLACES

IF YOU CURRENTLY EAT OUT A LOT, you may go into withdrawal if you try and cut down, but there's a high probability that what you are missing isn't the food so much as the 'third place' factor. This neat little term describes a place that is not work or home, but a *third* kind of place where you feel at ease, and a part of the greater world.

Town squares serve this function beautifully in many cultures where they are used as a staple of the community's 'going out' life. People set themselves up on a bench to watch the passing crowds, or take a leisurely stroll arm in arm, pausing to chat when they pass acquaintances. Teenagers get all teenagery in giggly group huddles, glancing excitedly over their shoulders to see who could be glancing back. You might buy a cob of roasted corn on a stick, or a handful of grain to scatter to the pigeons, but it's not obligatory. You feel refreshed by having been in the world, and stopping to drink it in. There are very few obvious non-commercial substitutes in your average western city.

It took your authors some practice to establish a repertoire of non-spending-oriented third places. We very much like our local park, which is used heavily by the surrounding community, and we often go lounge there at sunset and exchange pleasantries with people and their dogs. Maybe we bring a beer and a bag of peanuts. Maybe we don't. It feels like a proper third place occasion though, and it costs zero to ten bucks.

The library serves beautifully as a third place too. When the weather is bad it is positively luxurious to go hunker down in the temperature-controlled environment for an afternoon, writing, reading or gazing idly at the humans, speculating about their lives. Perhaps you bump into an angular old man (why do you feel like you've seen his face somewhere before…?) and he drops a book titled *101 Evil Uses for Cat Souls*. You try to hand it back to him, but he merely pushes rudely past you. Minutes later, you hear a scream that is unmistakably that of Mrs Finnegan the head librarian. Where *is* Sergeant Caper the library cat anyway you wonder? And why is there blood on my – Sorry! We just got this book muddled with the feline murder mystery we're also currently working on…

The beach is another great third place, as is a well-used community garden, but you can definitely get more creative. We had a mid-winter date in a laundromat once, after noticing what a great view of the streetscape the big windows offered. A little picnic, the warmth of the dryers, classic hits FM radio for a pleasingly dubious soundtrack, and an endless stream of passing humanity to provoke philosophical pontifications. Smashing.

As fond as your authors' memories of that evening are, its occurrence does tend to bring home how lacking in easily-identifiable, free, communal spaces many modern cities are. You may have an even more challenging time finding one if you live in a rural area – although if you can nurse a drink for an hour or so, the country pub can be a better cheap social space than you'd find in most big cities. Check out the pointers in the box below and see if you can come up with any more. If you can't, why not start one of your own? Your local council may even be prepared to help.

While it's definitely tricky to find public spaces that meet all the above criteria, your authors have noticed that it's possible to somewhat satiate the urge to 'be in the world, and gazing comfortably at it', in other ways. Choose to focus on your surroundings rather than on a handheld electronic device while travelling on public transport, or while waiting for a friend on the steps of a public building. Do a spot of people-watching, look at the tops of buildings and trees, let your brain be loose. Walk more slowly down the street, and survey the sights. Simply by sitting back and looking outwards, we can replicate the mental state we are chasing when we go into public spaces and pay for something as an excuse to feel leisurely there.

Doesn't this sound tops?

Ray Oldenberg, who coined the term, says a good third place should include the following characteristics:

- ~ cheap or free
- ~ easy to get to for many
- ~ welcoming and comfortable
- ~ occupants have little or no obligation to be there
- ~ no emphasis on anyone's social or economic status
- ~ both new and familiar faces should be found there
- ~ a playful mood, where conversation is the main activity
- ~ feels like a home away from home

We're willing to bet fifty of our seldom-squandered dollars that half of the world's psychologists would go out of business if there were more places like this.

16. DON'T THINK ABOUT MONEY

THIS BOOK HAS TO DO WITH MANY THINGS, and one of them is definitely money. Most books with anything to say about improving your relationship with money will tell you that you need to keep budgets and spreadsheets of your earnings and expenditure. This is no doubt dead necessary for some people who are in a tangle of debt or a financial pickle of some other form. We'd also recommend it as a revealing short-term experiment if you're the sort who frequently peers into the leathery crevasses of your wallet and wonders just where all that money got to, and so quickly too! If you are either of these people, you likely already think, and even worry, about money a fair bit.

The utterly beautiful news we have for you is that for most folk who have made habits of minimal consumption second nature, money is something they rarely think about. This was one of the more shocking constants your authors observed when talking to Frugal Hedonist friends – somehow even *we* had been somewhat sucked into the stereotype of the penny-pinching miser sitting up all night counting coins by the light of a grubby candle stub.

It is magnificent how it works: you operate on the general basis that you don't go shopping for entertainment, and you mostly just buy stuff you really need or value. You repair, repurpose, borrow and share things, buy fresh produce in season, take packed lunches, (we'll stop there before we paraphrase this entire book within one of its own sentences – like some kind of conceptual babushka doll) and the spare money just seems to gently accumulate.

It's actually a gorgeously exploitable paradox of living in a first world culture. Our wages are set to enable a 'basic standard of living' that is more than basic, so if you can get good at livin' large on *actual* basics, you end up with more money than you know what to do with! Then you get to come up with something to do with it, and that part is very nice too.

Thinking about money sounds annoying and dull. Worrying about money does not look fun at all. According to research it breaks up lots of relationships and raises blood pressure and all manner of other horrible things. Personally, we would much rather worship our bicycles, eat more baked potatoes, have two (okay, three) pairs of jeans, and take very long holidays in warm climates.

17. REVEL IN THE GOOD BRAIN CHEMISTRY OF RESOURCEFULNESS

WE MET LAWRENCE through the couch surfers' website. He said he could fix just about anything, and true to his word when he first turned up, after midnight, he immediately began repairing Adam's ancient bicycle light, even managing to rewire a miniscule broken bulb. The bulb was worth about 50c. It was clear that Lawrence wasn't fond of waste. And he had a MacGyver-esque compulsion to be resourceful. Lawrence, it turned out, lived almost entirely without money. He traded his formidable plumbing, electrical and carpentry skills for board and whatever else he needed. If it wasn't for his almost pathological affection for bad puns ("Are there any other kind?" ponders Adam. "He was quite a *pun*dit of the art wasn't he though?" quips Annie with glee), he would have been the perfect houseguest.

Lawrence had taken to extremes one of the seldom-acknowledged perks of frugality: a life liberally strewn with satisfying mini-challenges. Surveying your stash of scrap wood and pieces of glass and tin, and figuring out how to build that greenhouse you've wanted for so long. Darning your first ever sock and feeling chuffed that you just turned something broken into something useful. Getting the alchemy of a homemade loaf of bread just right. (Find links to help you do all these things and more in our Further Resources section!)

Your authors have noticed that these kind of accomplishments seem to induce in the problem-solver a surge of pleased/proud feelings very similar to those of solving a sudoku, or getting to the next level on a computer game. Only with the added bonus of knowing that you just made some *real stuff* better.

Everyday life used to provide people with ample opportunity to experience the satisfaction of being canny, constructive, and creative to achieve an end, via the constant necessity of making things and repairing or repurposing them. Apparently, this feeling is so pleasurable that as those necessary activities which supplied it have dwindled, we have invented leisure activities to supply it in their place – cutting up brand new fabric to use for recreational quilting, finding 'shed' projects to tinker on, building model aeroplanes, doing puzzles, gaming. We could even include sports in this list if we expand our definition of 'mini-challenges' to include drawing on *physical* resourcefulness to navigate and conquer a conundrum.

According to Hungarian psychology professor Mihaly Csikszentmihalyi, the good buzz you get from these kinds of activities comes as much from the process as from the outcome. He's the man who coined the term 'flow' to describe the state we can enter when performing a task that is within our capabilities, but is sufficiently challenging that our skills are exercised close to their limits. We experience flow (also known as 'being in the zone') when an activity so fully engages our attention that we get lost in the moment. And while this book focuses largely on sensual and social pleasures, your authors would hazard to suggest that 'flow' is an even more satisfying form of enjoyment.

If flow were a drug, it would be cocaine. According to flow researcher Corinna Peifer, a flow experience resembles the more positive aspects of a cocaine high: "a rewarding feeling of high energy and alertness, accompanied by an improvement of concentration (and therefore performance), a carefree trust in one's own abilities ... while forgetting about basic human needs such as hunger or sleep." Yes, the old man obsessively restoring a Model-T engine in his shed, and the high-flying lawyer snorting coke in the courthouse bathroom may be chasing the same kind of high.

*How to fix about half of all mysterious problems that occur in electrical items:**

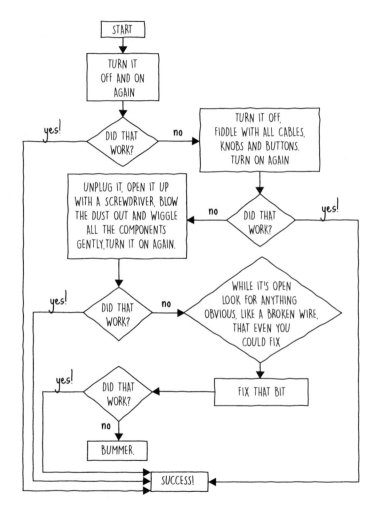

START

TURN IT OFF AND ON AGAIN

DID THAT WORK? — no → TURN IT OFF, FIDDLE WITH ALL CABLES, KNOBS AND BUTTONS. TURN ON AGAIN

yes! → SUCCESS!

DID THAT WORK? — no → UNPLUG IT, OPEN IT UP WITH A SCREWDRIVER, BLOW THE DUST OUT AND WIGGLE ALL THE COMPONENTS GENTLY, TURN IT ON AGAIN.

yes! → SUCCESS!

DID THAT WORK? — no → WHILE IT'S OPEN LOOK FOR ANYTHING OBVIOUS, LIKE A BROKEN WIRE, THAT EVEN YOU COULD FIX

yes! → SUCCESS!

FIX THAT BIT

DID THAT WORK? yes! → SUCCESS!

no → BUMMER.

* *Don't* try this with anything that contains massive capacitors (mainly old school cathode ray TVs) because they can give you a deadly shock even when unplugged.

While flow is most notably associated with making art, or navigating challenges within a sport, puzzle or game, frugal living gives you bountiful opportunity for similarly engrossing uses of your creative and physical abilities. Honing problem-solving skills so you can repair a motor or engine, developing an intuitive feel for cooking with raw ingredients, learning to draw for entertainment, becoming brilliantly nimble on your bicycle, training your foraging eye to lead you to bounty, getting good at crafting anything with your own hands – all these things take some perseverance while you're getting there, but once you're there, immersing yourself in using your skill is immensely, flow-ishly, pleasurable.

By the way beloved reader, we don't want to give you the impression that we're merely junkies for the fleeting flow-buzz here. For just as lovely as the instant surge of pleasure that comes from using your wits well, is the ravishing sense of freedom that comes with knowing that you have them there to be relied upon. The confidence that accompanies skills of self-reliance is a fine drug indeed – a drug of *in*dependence. And it just gets better the more you do it.

18. Grow your own greens

EVEN IF YOU HAVEN'T done much gardening before, or just aren't interested, we most fervently recommend growing your own salad and cooking greens, and perhaps some herbs.*

Here's why: leafy greens are some of the easiest, cheapest plants to grow, yet are expensive to store and transport, so are disproportionately expensive to buy. Home-grown and picked right before use, they are definitely tastier and more nutritious, not to mention pesticide-free. Greens generally don't need as much sunlight as many crops, don't take up much space, and can be grown very well in pots. Finally, you get to harvest just the amount you want, rather than paying for a whole bunch of thyme when you just needed a sprig, or a whole lettuce when you just wanted enough for a sandwich.

None of the above is as true for beetroot, carrots, onions, pumpkin, or most other crops. So for maximum kickbacks from your horticultural efforts, focus your talent, and become a Master of the Leaf.

Note: you may need to grow your greens in a raised bed if your suburb has a feral tortoise problem.

---

*   Almost anyone can find a good spot to grow parsley, mint, spring onions and chives. For Mediterranean herbs however (like rosemary, thyme, oregano, bay and sage), only go there if you can give them at least five hours of sunshine a day.

19. GET IN TOUCH WITH YOUR INNER HUNTER-GATHERER

IF IT SO HAPPENS THAT A DARK CLOUD HOVERS stubbornly over your green thumb, there is still one genre of plants you will likely excel at growing: *weeds*. This needn't be the curse it might seem, for the majority of leafy weeds are marvellous edible greens themselves. Amaranth, dandelion, mallow, purslane – even if you don't know the names, you're likely to recognise these globally ubiquitous pop-up plants. Most have been used in traditional cooking for thousands of years, and are actually more nutritious than cultivated plants.

Such a fine and fun skill is the hunt for wild greens that we have written a book on the topic (*The Weed Forager's Handbook*). As a bonus, if you make supplementing your diet this way a habit, you might just find that you have also begun to feed the fundamental *Homo sapiens* instinct to roam-and-pluck with something much more honest than another pair of shoes you really didn't need. While connecting with your ancestral cave-self, you may discover that you are connecting more intimately with your neighbourhood. The pursuit of wild foods not only furnishes you with a heightened awareness of the seasons, but has a way of leading you into corners of your garden or suburb that you would never have otherwise visited.

Here's one of our favourites to whet your appetite: purslane (Portulaca oleracea).
Use it like the Mexicans, cooked into scrambled eggs, or like the Greeks,
in a simple salad with tomatoes, red onion and parsley.

On one occasion, while out harvesting edible weeds on an overgrown vacant block, your authors grew languid and felt compelled to stop and lounge in the warm summer grass. Adam decided to use a large abandoned suitcase as a chair, then dozed off in its surprisingly comfortable embrace – a hazy magical experience tempered only slightly by waking up hours later feeling a little disoriented, cold, and abandoned, as Annie had long since headed home. Annie counters that Adam was looking so peaceful she couldn't possibly wake him, and anyway it's a nice neighbourhood, *and* she had food in the oven she had to go check on, and what is the whole point of this anecdote anyway? (Can we say at this point that co-authoring is a sometimes-challenging process…)

20. INDULGE YOUR CURIOSITY

PAPA HAS BROUGHT HOME PRESENTS from his trip to market! There is a hair ribbon, a piece of slingshot rubber, and a stick of hard candy which little Alice and Samuel carefully divide. Thrilling acquisitions to be sure, but just as thrilling is Papa's description of the orphaned baby kangaroo that the grocer's wife has taken on the care of. The children rain down questions about how it drinks its milk, where it sleeps, how long its tail is, and whether it has any fur yet. The answers are stashed away greedily for future contemplation.

Most people love the feeling of getting something new, but forget that it can come as easily from discovery as from consumption. A fascinating fact, a good anecdote, learning how to do something, having an experience you've never had before, hearing some gossip – *anything* that extends our picture of the universe we're part of.

Craving novelty or stimulation? Don't go buy another shirt or scan the papers for a new café to try. Instead, learn the name of three plants in your garden and what their Latin names mean. Use the internet to teach yourself a dance move. Read something by a writer you've always meant to get acquainted with. Take a free tour of a public building. Ask an eloquent friend to tell you about their childhood. Look up five uses for sour milk apart from the one listed in tip "5. Hate waste" of this book. Go to the library and find out the history of your suburb, street, or maybe even the past residents of your own home. Take a photo of the night sky every night for a fortnight, and see how it changes. Draw a picture of your cat… using your toes.

Indulging your curiosity isn't only a less expensive way of getting that 'Getting Feeling', it is deep hedonism. As your understandings amass, you begin to sense the world around you as a dense and majestic cathedral of thrumming, interconnected functions and stories. Plus, you can revel whole-heartedly in these riches as you accrue them, knowing that they require no wardrobe space or loan repayments!

This is a baby ladybird! It's not as pretty as its parents, but it sure eats a lot of aphids.

Knowledge can function in lieu of material goods in other ways too. Your authors would much rather someone showed up for afternoon tea bearing a piping hot tale of something riveting than clutching a bag of danishes, and we're certain many others feel the same way. Converting your thoughts or discoveries into something tellable not only entertains and enriches your audience, but it clarifies and cements them for you, the teller, too. You're forced to do a little ordering of the information in your head, noting its most crucial and captivating details. You might spot a few missing links that you'd like to fill in, or even a revelation you've come to. The whole process is an art well worth cultivating.

Indulging your curiosity can be as simple as diving for a dictionary every time you stumble across a word you don't know. Often, however, it drives you further afield, into the world of experience. Doing a long distance bike trip, eating a whole habanero chilli, experimenting with barefoot running, or going to midnight mass, all because you're *curious* what those things are like. Studies repeatedly indicate that experiences deliver more and longer lasting happiness than things do. (See our box under "37. Figure out what you really *do* enjoy spending money on" for more on this.)

Chasing experiential curiosity can be expensive, and is an area where your authors sometimes ignore frugality. We've forked out big bucks to take a hot air balloon trip, do a short course with a world-class expert, or go to a mind-blowing theatre show. We don't regret a penny of it though, not only because *most* of what we do to indulge our curiosity is free, but because being curious saves us from the costly compulsion to browse for new purchases as a source of stimulation and novelty.

We don't have a cat, so here are some pictures we drew of each other with our toes instead.

21. DON'T BE A SELFISH %$*#

NOT OVER-CONSUMING is simply the polite thing to do on a planet of finite resources. We will assume that you, dear reader, know a fair amount about this situation already, and have possibly even felt waves of paralysing doom crashing about you when contemplating the huge cogs of industry and economy that seem to churn relentlessly forward chomping up all that was sparkling and rich with energy and fertility stores laid down over millions and zillions of years. *Merde!*

Despite this awareness, most of us struggle to make the connection between our personal habits and this dismal situation in any visceral fashion. That's not surprising, given that the chains of supply and disposal enabling our consumption are now largely distant or hidden. For *most* of human history, we have been used to social and environmental setups where if we behave irresponsibly or greedily or lazily, life begins to suck: our neighbours shun us; our crops fail; all our assets go to pot; our animals die; our drinking water gets foul. Over time we have come to trust this mechanism that tells us that 'if life is really pleasant, then we can't be doing anything too bad'. So now, in this warped new setup, which enables us to *comfortably and repeatedly* do lazy, greedy things – causing really unimaginable harm – we just can't quite believe that our behaviour could be deeply problematic, because our living conditions are so freakin' pleasant.

Energy slaves

If you're an average English-speaking Westerner, and you were to power your current lifestyle with human muscle power (e.g., with slaves), how many people would you need? Answer: around 114 healthy slaves would have to work around the clock to move your car, heat your house and power your appliances. Thankfully, those lovely coalmines and oil wells mean we don't need to worry about pesky things like the welfare or uprisings of these 'energy slaves'. On the other hand, fossil fuels aren't turning out to be so trouble free either…

Don't be fooled though dear reader. Cause and effect are as real when it comes to personal consumption, as they were that time your poor high-school chemistry teacher made an inspired bid for your hormonally-distracted attention by dripping water onto powdered iodine and zinc, causing purple smoke to spew forth in a bat-out-of-hell way quite appealing to your melodramatic teenage aesthetics! Here are three examples of small personal behaviours that are cumulatively wreaking heinous death and destruction. Yet they could all be changed without even making a dent in our incredibly high standards of living. (The figures are from your authors' native Australia, but U.S. and U.K. stats are not so different.)

More than a third of all car trips in Australian cities are under three kilometres. Many of these are to supermarkets. Every time we permit ourselves this kind of driving (instead of walking, riding, or planning shopping around one trip a week instead of four) we produce unnecessary CO_2 and pollutants. You know, that stuff which is causing unseasonable droughts, floods, fires and hurricanes, and giving everyone respiratory disorders.

Many of us habitually set household thermostats a couple of degrees unnecessarily high in winter and low in summer (see also "44. Acclimatise to the seasons"), dumping even more CO_2 and pollutants into the atmosphere. Wearing woolly scarves and jumpers all winter may be a tad annoying, but then so is losing all your crops (if you're a farmer), and also having no ice to stand on any more (if you're a polar bear).

As a nation we not only overeat, but we each throw away an average of about 135 kilograms of food* per year. (See "5. Hate waste" for more on this.) This occurs via habits like not using leftovers, buying one-off ingredients for recipes, and eating out at restaurants where the exaggerated servings force the poor distended diner to leave half the food on their plate. This food equates to *millions* of tonnes of fertilisers mined and synthesised, not to mention all the water inputs and the oil and other resources used for processing, packaging and transport.

It's not as though any of us chose to be born into this distorted situation, where everything is arranged to encourage us to constantly consume beyond the planet's means. But that doesn't mean we can't do something about it. Like adopting the more streamlined consumption habits of a Frugal Hedonist. The sooner we do so, the less damage will be left behind, and the more eons-long pleasure, on a Whole-Planet-With-All-Its-Monkeys-And-Trees-And-Small-Albino-Whales level, there will be left to share.

---

*   It may seem like there is a lot of ranting in this book about the careless use of food. Here's why: for Australians, around 28% of our personal greenhouse gas emissions are created by the production and distribution of the food we buy (by comparison, electricity, gas heating and other energy used *directly* in the home only account for 16%). Over half of our personal water use also comes courtesy of the food system. In fact, these figures are underestimates, as they don't include driving to the shops or home refrigeration and cooking when assessing food's resource toll.

22. REMEMBER THE WORLD OF 1950S' SCI-FI

SOMETIMES YOUR AUTHORS like to think of frugality as a way for everyone to get what was once the expected result of mechanisation and labour-saving devices: more leisure time. For much of last century, people were very optimistic about this. It did seem likely, given the appearance on the scene of some nifty inventions which simplified daily tasks and increased comfort – electric lights, vacuum cleaners, quick-dry stretch textiles… "Surely", thought humanity, "we will now cease to ruin our eyes sewing by candlelight, reclaim those hours once spent pushing brooms around, and move about like gazelles in our light flexible clothing!"

Instead, there eventuated the paradox where we made doing stuff easier and faster, and then just developed ever-escalating standards of normalised consumption expectations, and more industries to cater to them. And that meant we had just as much work to do as ever.

Consuming less enables not only you, but your fellow humans, to work less. Imagine that when you buy a washing machine – what a fabulous invention – you buy a good quality one that lasts. You look after it, only wash your clothes when they are actually dirty, only use it when you have a full load, and use minimal eco-friendly detergent.

You have not only saved yourself money, but you have reduced the labour load of the people who mine the component materials, make, sell, and distribute washing machines. You have also shaved some time off the working day for the people at the waste water treatment plant, those doing environmental clean-up of ocean pollution problems, and those who dispose of white goods at the landfill site. Imagine this effect magnified via *all* your consumption choices! And if the people working in those industries were *also* consuming more frugally, it wouldn't matter that there was less work to be done sum total, because *they* wouldn't need to work so much either!

Unlike the smoggy *Blade-Runneresque* cityscapes anticipated by the sci-fi of the eighties, fifties' sci-fi veered more towards visions of verdant hills dotted with transparent pod dwellings under a crystal blue sky. Here again, doing less work can help us redirect back towards our utopian ideals. Data indicates that households with higher work hours have higher carbon footprints. Being time-stressed makes people behave in more carbon intensive ways (travelling faster, eating out more, doing more 'convenience' shopping). *Countries* with higher work hours have higher carbon footprints too – because of the time-stressed households that comprise them, and because more economic activity demands more resource use.

Just like ecological health, human health gets gradually eroded by keeping our noses glued too firmly to the grindstone. (And heaven knows your 1950s sci-fi utopia white tube suit won't look half as fetching with anxiety lines etched into your forehead... or type II diabetes giving you foot gangrene.) Long work hours are associated with elevated stress – now acknowledged to be so bad for our bodies and minds that prominent clinical investigator George P. Chronous estimates that it likely accounts for more than half of the US's healthcare-related expenses. The Japanese, notorious for their culture's intense work ethic, even have a word for death by overwork: *karōshi*.

Back in 1914, Henry Ford figured out that the 'the-more-hours-the-better' legacy of the industrial revolution (see our next tip "23. Swot up on the history of work") was actually damaging productivity in his car manufacturing plants. He slashed working hours, and dazzled by the profitable results, the rest of industry followed suit. Modern productivity researchers continue to confirm Ford's findings. They implore their corporate clients

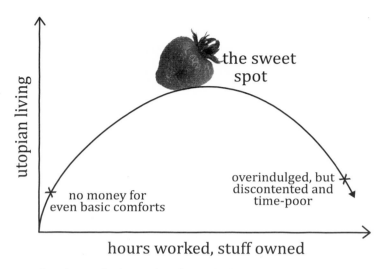

the sweet spot

utopian living

overindulged, but discontented and time-poor

no money for even basic comforts

hours worked, stuff owned

Frugal Hedonists think it is absurd to suffer from the living being too good.

to ensure that employees take frequent breaks, use up allocated holidays, and don't take work home, all for the sake of productivity. Strangely, no one seems as inclined to listen any more. Work hours have been climbing steadily in most English-speaking countries since the 1970s; weekends are an endangered concept, and 55 hour weeks, plus unpaid overtime, are the norm in many professions. Many European countries have taken a stand against such all-consuming work weeks. An average worker in Germany or the Netherlands, for example, works a whopping 400 fewer hours per year than their American counterpart. That's like getting ten standard working weeks of extra holiday time. Despite this, Germany manages to be the fourth largest economy in the world.

So. If it's not even the best way to get work done, *and* it's leading society away from our most utopian visions for our health, lifestyle and environment, why are we going along with this work-mad trend so meekly? Why aren't we all scratching our heads and saying "Hold on a minute, I think I'd like the version where the machines have us all doing *less* work please"?

Such a big question rarely has a single answer. One culprit is surely this culture we've created that equates having an insignificant work life with being a bit of a loser. This certainly seems a bad scene – when it comes to status, our glitchy psyches have a tendency to endlessly up the ante, meaning it becomes almost impossible to *ever* feel content with what we've achieved. So we strive and produce, without stopping to consider how necessary the products of our strivings really are.

Another factor may be those murky machinations of The Powers That Be. Some cultural commentators think that since a population whose lives are dominated by work is more docile, governments tend to gear policy towards this end – consciously or not. And that the corporation CEOs with whom our political leaders play golf have a similar agenda. As popular blogger David Cain puts it: "Keeping free time scarce means people pay a lot more for convenience, gratification, and any other relief they can buy. It keeps them watching television, and its commercials."

And then, of course, there is The Economy. That heffalump is perhaps the most oft-cited reason for why we need to keep 'creating jobs', working them, and shopping – whether or not there is work that needs to be done or things we need to buy. The problem here is that The Economy requests the absurd: endless growth on a planet of finite resources. Yes, The Economy would suffer if we all started working less. Even the drop in hospital visits for stress-fuelled diseases would register negatively with the GDP, as would the reduction in resources mined to keep office lights and photocopiers humming around the clock...

The point is, economic activity is fatally flawed as the measure of human success and happiness in the first place, so let's not shape our attitude to work around its needs. Let's shape it around how much work actually needs doing to keep us supplied with a few simple comforts – i.e, the kind that seemed luxurious only seventy years ago! Hello 1950s' dream of people lounging around in gardens sipping drinks chilled by those fabulous newfangled refrigerator things, wearing soft fabrics, and reading philosophy while playing footsies. (Sorry, no robot housemaid.)

Where we were headed vs. where we wound up

In the middle decades of the 20th century, the assumption that we would embrace the liberty offered by technological advancements was not limited to science fiction imaginings.

In 1930, evolutionary biologist Julian Huxley predicted a two-day work week. "The human being can consume so much and no more... When we reach the point when the world produces all the goods that it needs in two days, as it inevitably will, we must curtail our production of goods and turn our attention to the great problem of what to do with our new leisure." His contemporary, John Maynard Keynes, was similarly concerned by what all this leisure would mean: "Man will be faced with ... how to use his freedom from pressing economic cares, how to occupy the leisure, which science and compound interest will have won for him." In his 1956 presidential nomination speech, Dwight D. Eisenhower described a future where "leisure ... will be abundant, so that all can develop the life of the spirit, of reflection, of religion, of the arts, of the full realization of the good things of the world." A 1965 US Senate subcommittee predicted that by the year 2000 Americans would be working 14 hours a week, with at least seven weeks of vacation time annually.

Obviously, something went astray en route to this seemingly inevitable hammock-fest. In her bestseller, *The Overworked American*, Juliet B. Schor points out that the productivity of the U.S. worker has more than doubled since 1948, meaning that: "we could actually have chosen the four-hour day... But between 1948 and the present, we did not use any of the productivity dividend to reduce hours."

Today, there is a growing movement questioning if the weird path we took instead was the right one. Could we reclaim what we thought we had coming with a gradual re-jigging of the work-consumption-life balance? Many very clever people seem to think so. Some of them are involved in the New Economics Foundation's 21 Hours campaign, which advocates cutting the standard working week down to 21 hours. If you'd like to hear their most eloquent reasoning, have a look at the URLs in our Further Resources section.

23. SWOT UP ON THE HISTORY OF WORK

EVEN IF YOU COULDN'T GIVE A RAT'S BELLYBUTTON for the economy, or a goose's toot for having an enviable career, all this talk of deliberately working less might still sit uncomfortably with you. Paid work, in our culture, is considered both the activity in which most of life will naturally be spent, and a virtue. Is this simply the fundamental way of the world, or are there other ways to think about things? How did we arrive at *this* way in the first place?

From the late 16th to 18th centuries European moral value systems took a heavy re-moulding by Protestantism, with its emphasis on work as the focal point of life and the road to salvation. Forswearing pleasure and frivolity was encouraged, and the attainment of money was seen as a sign that you were making fine headway into God's good books. Large portions of society have *had* to work hard for millennia, but now work became something to be pursued for its own noble sake.

The industrial revolution followed hot on the heels of this shift, and with its gluttonous need for labour to operate its new factories, was more than happy to have religion encouraging a strong work ethic in the poorer classes. A fervour for progress became the motif of the newly respectable merchant class, and was celebrated in media and morality alike. In 1783, industrialist Josiah Wedgwood – the man behind the crockery – embodied the spirit of the age by applauding "well directed and long continued ... exertions, both in masters and servants," these behaviours being "very good in keeping my eleventh commandment – *thou shalt not be idle.*"

A Wedgewood vase decoration. Idleness was obviously okay with Josiah after all – provided it remained strictly within the confines of art.

This period of sweat and ambition generated several technologies that ultimately improved living conditions for millions. But it also so firmly entrenched the idea that it is The-Inevitable-Lot-Of-Humankind-To-Labour-In-Servitude-To-Development-And-Expansion, that previous attitudes towards work were effectively lost. Given how many of us feel like we might have had enough Development And Expansion for the time being thank you very much, your authors figure that some of those older attitudes might be worth revisiting…

Travelling first to the times of our hunter-gatherer forebears, we find them largely without words for work. Criminy! Does this indicate a life of such incessant toil that no other state was imaginable?! Not at all: mid 20th century studies of hunter-gatherer groups living in a traditional manner put their average 'work' day – that is, taking care of necessary tasks – at under five hours. Many of these tasks were also social and playful, and so probably felt far-removed from wage slave drudgery.

Most pre-modern societies seem to have had no word for work either. The ancient Greeks didn't, and so could speak of work only in the negative. When Aristotle is quoted as having observed that "We work in order to achieve leisure", what he actually wrote was closer to this: "We are *un-leisurely* in order to achieve leisure." Either translation suggests that work itself was not viewed as a thing of much intrinsic value in ancient Greece.

One modern stigma around eschewing work is its association with the ludicrously-privileged aristocracy of the old European class system. Yet the medieval lower classes seemed no more ideologically driven to less-than-necessary work than the gentry. While toil was certainly hard and long in areas where agricultural conditions (or your feudal lords) were tough, there are also indications that peasant life could be quite a romp.

Records from 15th century France, for example, show that an average of one day out of every four was an official holiday, frequently of a kind that meant carnival and revelries for the peasantry. In Essex in the 14th century casual labourers are estimated to have worked no more than 120 days a year, and not for lack of opportunity. Barbara Ehrenreich writes in *Dancing in the Streets: A History of Collective Joy* that "the period from the thirteenth to the fifteenth century can be seen … as one long outdoor party, punctuated by bouts of hard labor."

The artisan classes appear also to have been free of any moral compunction towards non-essential labour; a fact distressing to more pious types as the cogs of the industrial age got grinding. John Houghton, a commentator on trade, bemoaned in 1681 the lack of labour put in by knitters and makers of silk stockings as soon as they "had a great price for their work", and described them as spending "most of their time at the ale-house or nine-pins … as long as they have a penny of money."

Let's stop there, and rest our reeling heads! We don't know about you, but your authors actually go a bit wonky over the concept of doing just enough paid work to pay for basic needs, and then treating time as a malleable substance to be shaped – even aimlessly squandered – as we please. We struggle to untether ourselves from the idea that ongoing achievement is essential for a worthwhile life. But what if it's not? Our flit through history hints that achievement could be an overrated, relatively modern habit. Maybe it would be just fine to spend much, much more time looking around at the world, going cross-country orienteering through our own fascinating minds, and enjoying those of other humans.

Beloved reader, we are the first to admit that some work feels like a marvellous use of time. We have earned money doing many truly rewarding things;

Peasants drinking (detail) by Adriaen van Ostade (circa 1676)

things where we were stimulated by learning and thinking, meeting riveting people, creating stuff we were proud of, journeying to unusual locations. But we don't think that anyone should spend most of life working without questioning the whole equation first. So we suggest taking a step back from the blackboard, the better to view the tales from history chalked up there for your rumination. Put yourself in a cocktail shaker with them, and mix their globules up with your globules. Then have a ponder.

Bonus bonuses of working less

~ Even if you love your work, you will probably love it even more if you don't feel hedged into doing it *x* hours a week, *x* weeks a year, ad infinitum.

~ If you *don't* love your work, reducing your hours can allow you to appreciate its good bits – sociability, or the way it keeps you fit or takes you to places that you wouldn't otherwise go. Even a job you thought you hated can sometimes become enjoyable when you do it less – you actually didn't hate the job, but how much it dominated your life.

~ Working less almost always saves you money. You might spend less on work-related expenses (transport, clothes that you don't wear anywhere else, an up-to-the-minute iPad you feel you can't do without). You might spend less on de-stressing (yoga classes, remedial alcohol or therapy bills). You might be able to give up some 'busy-ness enablers', like frequent takeaway food, time-saving appliances, or even a car.

Of course, whittling down your working life isn't always as straightforward as asking for fewer shifts per week. For some people it will require serious life overhauls: restructuring or job-sharing your role, volunteering for a demotion or changing careers. If you're fettered by serious mortgage or car repayments, it might mean moving to a smaller house, or to an area with better public transport.

24. Bring a bag

ERM, WE'RE NOT REALLY SURE how much more needs saying on this one. Take a bag with you when you go places. It enables you to carry two excellent money-savers: a water bottle and food from home. A person without a bag is at the mercy of using their wallet to obtain anything they might need throughout the day.

If you buy something, you can put that in your bag too, so you don't have to use a plastic one. (Okay, go ahead and nominate us for a 'most obvious statement of the year' award.) Some people keep another bag inside their regular bag. Like one of those thin fabric shopping bags that stuff inside themselves to form an improbably small cushion. That way, if they buy a lot of watermelon *and* a lot of mangoes all at the same time, they still have enough bag. Easy.

A pocket is really a cloth-ing-attached bag, seen here reaching its zenith in a suit once worn by comedian Bill Oddie. When Adam was a youngster he imagined that, in the future, everyone would be prepared for any eventuality by wearing suits like this.

25. NOTICE WHEN YOU HAVE ENOUGH

A WHILE BACK ANNIE MADE A LIST that looked like this:

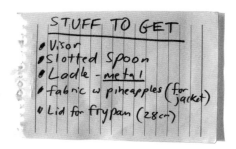

STUFF TO GET
- Visor
- Slotted Spoon
- Ladle - metal
- fabric w pineapples (for jacket)
- Lid for frypan (28cm)

She acquired a pan lid (from a box of kitchen gear someone had put out on the street) and a visor (via a friend's closet-purge) before she got around to cruising the second-hand stores. When she did go, she quickly found a perfect ladle and slotted spoon, put them in her basket, and went to hunt for pineapple-patterned clothing (futilely – the drought in pineapple-print textiles out there is truly severe, and Annie resorted to embroidering pineapples onto her jacket while being read stories by Adam over some long winter evenings).

Approaching the cash register, Annie felt an odd aversion to buying the two utensils. A little voice in her head was saying, 'Life has actually been great without those things in it for *years* now, so why get them? Sure, you put them on a list because there were a couple of times where you thought, "What we need right now is a slotted spoon." But you got around it just fine on those occasions, and you will continue to get around it on any such future occasions.' She returned the utensils to the shelf, and left the store empty handed, which felt surprisingly nice. The two utensils would've cost a grand total of $1.98, so it definitely wasn't price that prevented her from buying them. It was the pleasant lightness that came with recognising her true lack of need for them.

We can spend a lot of energy in modern life tallying up what we might be lacking. Most people carry a conscious or subconscious 'Things would be better if...' list in their heads, which they constantly update and revise. It can be phenomenally liberating to notice that your life has been fine so far, maybe even pretty damn good, with what you already have. (Or that if it hasn't, it's probably *not* because of a deficit of wireless speakers or a proper toothbrush holder instead of that mug with the pictures of Smurfs on it that you've always used to keep toothbrushes in.)

So, the question you might want to ask yourself next time you are about to buy something (whether it's a slotted spoon or a whole new kitchen), is not 'Will this make my life better?' but 'Has my life so far been bad without this in it?'

This line of questioning circumvents some common bugs in the human brain. In most cases a new purchase *does* make some small aspect of life easier or nicer, and our brains anticipate this without factoring in the complete

price of our purchases – be it money-stress, over-stuffed cupboards, reduced creativity, or getting pudgy. Our brains also generally fail to acknowledge how speedily we will adapt to our slightly improved life and start scanning for the next thing that could be bettered, barely pausing to register a happiness spike from the previous improvement. By comparison, just the act of asking yourself the second question can make you feel happier, as you notice with shock how well-off you really are!

A crucial step in allowing this mental process to happen is to put a little time between the idea of buying something and actually doing it. If you're merely *thinking* that you should get something, you can put it through this filter any old time. If you're already in a store surging with the adrenaline of an imminent impulse buy, take a deep breath, step away from the throw rug/shoes of the moment/wooden duck/milk-frother, and go about your day. Still convinced that you should buy the Object of Desire a week later? Go back and get it. Mostly you will have forgotten about it by then, and gotten on with more interesting things.

More good is not always better

It's not just our gear that we tend to assume we should improve if we have the capacity to. Humans feel a strong compulsion to say 'yes' to anything our culture has deemed Good, from a promotion (even if we already feel overwhelmed at work) to an all-expenses paid trip to speak at a conference in Barcelona (even if we are already way too busy for comfort). Frugal Hedonism is partly about noticing when less might be more, and that applies to activity just as much as in the realm of consumption. If you're too busy, don't add a new commitment unless you can ditch a current one. If you're already loving life, check whether saying yes to another appealing project could steal important time from some less visible aspects of your world. It's as much about the spaces between things as it is about the things themselves, man…

26. Reinvent Christmas

YOUR AUTHORS REALISE it only happens once a year, but we reckon that reinventing Christmas is useful because it is so emblematic: if *Christmas* can be improved via frugality, then *anything* can.

It's been over ten years since Annie told everyone she knew that she didn't want any Christmas presents and wouldn't be giving any. She made an exception for her one remaining grandma, said granny being old enough to maybe not quite get it (and also old enough to have done a lot of frugal-time herself, enabling her to really appreciate small gifts like a box of Turkish delight). Those merry souls who choose to vanquish Christmas consumption mania often make a similar exception for children, but keep the presents humble in scale. Perhaps a stocking filled with small treasures: packets of glitter, a book, novel trinkets (curly straws, a magnifying glass, chocolate coins), or craft materials – perfect for allowing the grown-ups to relax all day while the stocking's contents are explored and put to use.

Find the consumption grotesque, but would still like to give something? What about only giving non-material presents (like a voucher for a massage, a lesson of some kind, or an afternoon of professional housecleaning). We know one circle of friends who decided to each make a donation to a charity at Christmas instead of giving each other presents. If you want to keep it small and yet stay away from useless tokenistic stuff, why not put aside a selection of the year's best homemade preserves and pickles to serve as gifts? People love pickles! Such treats also have the advantage of a long shelf life, meaning they create no sense of obligation to eat even *more* food over Christmas.

For many people, festive food is another area of consumption-induced strain, and The Perfect Christmas Meal becomes an exhausting marathon of shopping and preparation, leaving (usually) the woman of the house so busy getting a parade of dishes to the table that she barely gets to sit down and enjoy them. And this over-catering scarcely makes sense in an age and culture where most people feel like they eat too much on a regular basis.

In eras when daily fare was very humble and featured virtually no 'treat' foods, a feast was anticipated with legitimate glee, typically including more animal protein, and energy-dense luxuries like dried fruit and honey. But we live in an age where meat is left to spoil in thousands of refrigerators across the country daily, hamburgers and milkshakes are thrown away half consumed, and dried fruit is considered a virtuous alternative to snacking on cookies. This excess-on-top-of-excess can lead to yet *more* Christmassy stress, as attempts to resist over-indulging at a parade of festive season work bashes and family gatherings segue seamlessly into guilt and dismayed resolutions to get to the gym more often to work off the 'holiday bulge'.

What's the alternative? If you're feeding people, you could focus on quality instead of quantity to avoid ending up with piles of excess food. Make a regular-sized meal but base it around scrumptious seasonal and local ingredients or an old family recipe – food that has atmosphere and stories behind it. Decorate the table; make a big deal out of eating. Or invert the whole tradition and have carpet picnic of nothing but champagne, turkey and cranberry sauce toasted sandwiches, and chocolates, while the whole family plays word games. The kids will love it, and there'll be hardly any washing up. If someone else is hosting you, don't just bring an extra dish because you feel like it's The Done Thing – offer to help cook or clean up instead. And if you've been specifically asked to bring something, avoid over-catering by asking the cook which part of the meal they'd like you to provide.

So forget cramming-in shopping after work, paying off Christmas credit card debt, and sensing that you may be ill if you eat one more box of mediocre fudge that someone gave you because they felt like they 'had to get you *something*'. Take Christmas into your own hands, and mould it into something admirable. A frugal Christmas is the anti-stress, brandy-laced event a holiday should be. Imagine a delicious few days off, spending time with your clan, cooking together, making up stupid games, and having very long afternoon naps.

A typical modern American Christmas scene

By contrast, the above line up of presents had Laura and Mary in Little House on The Prairie *quite dizzy with excitement: a tin cup, a penny, a small cake and a candy cane.*

27. BE A CHARACTER

OKAY, NO PRESSURE HERE. This is far from an essential step to frugality, but having more *personality* is a seriously excellent substitute for constructing a *persona* via consumption patterns (like what you own, wear, eat and drive; where you live and holiday). You don't have to become one of those old men who get about in bare feet and a pinstripe suit with a six-foot python wrapped about their necks, but you do have to hone-in on things you're interested in and pursue them, develop your own opinions, or let some of those quirks and eccentricities that you may have been suppressing blossom into visible traits. People love to gossip, so give them that gift by being worthy of it! Cultivate blithe disregard for a couple of your least favourite cultural conventions – it makes people feel less embarrassed about their own shortfalls by comparison! Be simultaneously stupendous in some other regards, and you've got yourself a package.

Having a degree of social standing is important to all humans, whether they admit it or not (and is actually an important part of being successfully frugal - see also "30. People who need people..."). There are more ways than one to pickle that particular hedgehog however, and earning a place amongst your fellow humans via Who You Are, rather than How Neatly You Fit In, is highly effective, and often much cheaper.

28. IT WON'T BE DULL. WE PROMISE.

IT'S EASY TO ASSUME that living without spending much will be all samey and unstimulating and lonesome. Gather round, dear readers, and let Annie tell you a tale of a poor village in the wilds of Transylvania…

A couple of years ago I spent some time on a farm in a small, self-reliant Romanian village, and was utterly astonished by the degree of socialising taking place daily. I had envisioned life in a traditional agrarian society to be defined by days of long repetitive toil off in some field. Perhaps a bit of a chinwag or a knees-up at the end of the day to relieve the boredom, *if* you had enough energy left or could get your hands on some grog. But, while work in Reghin did occupy most of the day, it was not only diverse, but so chock-full of wheeling, dealing and problem solving that it felt more like bouts of vigorous exercise interspersed with gregarious socialising.

A sample day might consist of rising at dawn to collect eggs, only to discover that the goats have nudged the bar out of the stall door and escaped to graze a neighbour's field instead of waiting to be tethered near the brambles you wanted them to eat. A mad goat chase through the dewy field ensues, and the neighbour helps catch the goats, then returns with us to the house to discuss the extent of the damage done. Coffee is drunk, and sweet bread (in homage to the neighbour's presence at the table) is produced in place of the usual corn porridge. Some outrageous flirting goes on between the adolescents who have wandered in to see if anyone is eating anything good, and an offer is made to transport the neighbour's excess roosters to market that week (to smooth over the goat incident perhaps). Everyone eats and laughs, and once the visitors leave we set off to hoe the field up the road in preparation for potatoes.

On the way we have to stop and lean on the fence posts of every field we pass to exchange lewd jokes (mostly constructed around husbands and wives and livestock), to update old bargains and strike new ones, and to be accused of being drunk – since we thought chasing goats might be a better way to greet the dawn than making corn porridge. After three hours hoeing, overlaid by much yelling of jokes and arguing about politics (and interrupted at one point by a man appearing from the forest behind us with three huge poles he has cut to give to us because he has seen wolves in the forest just that morning and they are hungry and we may need to fend them off) we walk back to the house for lunch.

A destitute old lady is waiting in front of the house. Apparently she was once from a very good family, but they are all dead now, so she walks around asking for charity from different people each day. She can't make it up the front steps, so we carry the table outside, and bring our fried cabbage and onions and corn porridge out to eat with her. We walk back along the street (more banter along the way) to continue our hoeing, but a rainstorm suddenly sweeps in so we gather up tools and sprint back to the house to sort bean seed from last season while chatting and listening to fuzzy pop songs on the radio for a few hours.

A neighbour's small son prances through the mud to announce that we're wanted to inspect the progress of a ploughshare his dad is fixing for us. We dash down the road under a tarpaulin held aloft, and after agreeing on how to proceed with the repairs we meander into an extended conversation about town goings-on, how many violinists will be needed for the onion festival next week, and when the cherries will ripen this year. In fact, perhaps the blacksmith would like to be paid in cherry brandy for fixing the ploughshare? Should we just pop home now and get some for him to sample to help him make his mind up? We do, and we all drink some cherry brandy, and the blacksmith brings out poppyseed cake to accompany it. As we finally make our exit, he suggests that we might like some help pulling the hay out of our barn loft. We accept his offer, and after we all finish the job, he sweeps up a barrow full of hay to feed the horse he is keeping in our spare stall.

We visit a lady at the end of the village (more banter en route) who apparently grows the best vegetable seedlings, and incredibly, stay only long enough to collect the seedlings, help her coax her husband, who is a drunkard, back into bed, chop some wood for her (as everyone knows that the husband is no use for such things), and philosophise with her about the nature of alcoholism and the fact that she manages things better without him anyway.

We spend several manic hours attempting to get all 500 tomato seedlings into the ground before dark, and just make it in time to feed, water, and shut up all the animals. We are out of bread, so after washing ourselves and putting on warmer clothes, we stroll through the village night dotted with yellow lamplit windows and the melody of the creek's rain-swollen gurgling, and spend half an hour loitering by the shop-which-is-also-the-pub counter, catching up on any events of the day that we are yet to hear of, and being regaled with tales of trees that collect gold around their roots by one of the old men in the corner.

We leave with our bread, and also some sugar to take to the shepherds up in the mountains who are looking after our sheep for the season. If this rain continues, the path up the mountain will grow boggy, so it is best if we hike up there tomorrow with the anti-tick medicine they need for our sheep. And they will appreciate sugar and also some onions from our garden to go with all the fresh cheese they will feed us. Back home we drink a large beer, talk, cook, eat, and sleep.

COMFORTABLY AS RICH A DAY as one spent going to work and then going out to dinner and a movie with some friends afterwards.

You may consider this narrative to be largely irrelevant to your own life, given the culture and location in which it takes place. But read on, beloved reader, for the three tips to follow focus precisely on how mixing the practical with the social, and not sourcing all that you need via purchasing power, can help to create a lifestyle dense with frugal diversity no matter where you live…

29. DO BUSINESS WITH FRIENDS

THE POPULARITY OF THE PHRASE 'Don't do business with friends' seems a particularly modern indulgence. Obviously such a saying can only arise in an economic system where we actually have the option of keeping our financial and practical interactions at arm's length (along with any conviviality or conflict that may accompany them). More troublingly, the phrase indicates a lack of confidence in our capacities to communicate clearly, stand up for ourselves, forgive others, and acknowledge our own mistakes.

Adam runs a permaculture education and design business with a long-term friend. Over time, customers have turned into friends, and in some cases, even joined the business. Culinarily-talented friends are hired to cater for workshops, putting more love (and home grown produce) into the food than any professional caterer could. Potentially delicate issues with suppliers have been resolved while passing around bottles of homebrew and plates of roasted Fred... Fred being a cow raised by the business's warehouse manager. Adam wouldn't advise going into business with just anyone you hang out with, especially when your taste in company favours reckless and rebellious characters. But given the initial application of a bit of finer judgement, he finds there to be something truly unique about the camaraderie of a good working friendship. Socialising plus plus.

Annie did this painting in return for a friend insulating her shed. She knew it would take twice as long to do as the work on the shed would, but it still felt like a fair deal, because she'd be forced to pick up her oil paints again – something she knew she'd enjoy.

Annie chooses to do as much of her business with friends as possible. She reckons that it keeps her reasonable and honest. Behave poorly, and it will come directly back to her via ill feeling from people she sees all the time. Communicate poorly and she risks feeling let down by people she cares about. So she rents out rooms to friends in the house she amicably co-owns with her ex-husband (and is paying off with help from a loan from her mum). She pays unemployed friends to help her repaint her house. She can only afford a crummy hourly rate but sweetens it by providing lunch, fine repartee, and a scintillating soundtrack of 80s' mixtapes. She trades plants for car-favours, compost worms for singing lessons, garden designs for home repairs, editorial services for massages. She has sold paintings to friends and sewn costumes for their theatrical performances. Of course there have been disagreements along the way, but she has never once lost a friendship or maintained a grievance, and has shared many more layered experiences than she would have if it was all just pure sociability, or if the exchanges had been purely monetary.

Joking and teasing are essential for maintaining mutual tolerance in such dealings. Stating the terms of any agreement at the start is crucial. Don't be bashful about naming your price or engaging in playful barter with a friend – if you know you're playing fair, there's nothing to feel awkward about. Honest confessions early in the piece of possibly unreasonable but non-negotiable personal pedantries are helpful too: "I realise it's loco, but I'm a little obsessed about painting the tops of the door frames too. I know they're up there." Particularly useful is the recognition that as long as everyone is happy, exactitude is not as valuable as it is sometimes made out to be. A deal elegantly-struck, rather than pedantically-struck, can leave both parties feeling clever and content.

Doing the kind of business with friends that is based on trade rather than money has a couple of extra special perks. Often both parties can trade something that they consider easy to give. It may be a skill that they find enjoyable to use, or something they don't need, or have a surplus of. Not many people feel that way about money. The real icing on the cake is that by challenging money's role as the fundamental unit of practical transactions, we expand our capacity to see value in *other* things in life that come to us without the use of money. And that way doth great riches lie…!

30. People who need people are the luckiest people in the world

Beyond sociable business and barter, lies the even-less-formal informal economy. A.K.A. the gift economy, reciprocity, social credit. This is where you do helpful stuff for people, mostly because it feels right*, but probably also with an underlying sense that what goes around, comes around.

This reciprocity can be direct and conscious (bringing a bag of excess apples as a token of your appreciation to the neighbour who helped you find your lost puppy), or much more diaphanous and subconscious. Perhaps you have a friend who you've always lent your chainsaw to when he needed one.

---

* Apparently, it also feels right to your body. A plethora of research on social connectedness shows that feeling like a member of a strong social and functional community – get ready for it – improves your antibody response, lowers your cortisol (stress hormone) levels, improves sleep, slows physiological aging, improves recovery after coronary heart surgery, decreases depression, mortality, morbidity, and obesity. Shazam!

One day you mention that your old computer has given up the ghost, and because he was planning to upgrade his anyway, he decides to do it sooner rather than later, and gives his old laptop to you instead of trying to hawk it on eBay. In all likelihood he doesn't consciously view this as a reciprocal act for all those years of chainsaw lending, but because you inhabit a place in his brain associated with generosity, he feels good about helping you out.

Your authors have noticed a popular presumption hanging about, that being able to pay for whatever you need, so that you don't have to rely on anybody else, is a Most Desirable State Of Affairs. But as with so many things, *the dose makes the poison*: a measure of financial independence is convenient, but make money the dominant mode by which you satisfy needs and wants, and you start missing out on a whole lotta living. You can also become quite a lonely grouch.

> **Scene 1a.** Your family is moving house, but you don't have a car or the budget for a removalist service. You organise three different friends to each do a carload or two with you over the course of a week. You make sure your cooking stuff gets there on the first night, and cook a huge batch of stew, and each night you have dinner with the friends who've just helped you, sitting on make-do furniture in your new living room. One of these friends has a superb aesthetic eye, and as you pour her a second glass of the wine you've bought to demonstrate your gratitude, the muse strikes and she suggests several clever ways you could tart-up your new house cheaply and easily. Another friend insists on staying on after dinner to help you unpack boxes, and after stumbling across your childhood photo album you both wind up telling your kids stories about when you were their age – they even seem gratifyingly riveted. By the end of the week, all your stuff is moved, and the house already feels like a home from the presence of so many people eating and laughing there.

> **Scene 1b.** Your family is moving house, and you hire a removalist service to come shift the lot.

> **Scene 2a.** You are cruising down Main Street in a tiny country town, looking out for the turn-off to the house of a friend who recently

moved there. There is hardly a street sign to be seen, so you pull up alongside an old man sitting on a bench with what turns out to be a rooster in a cardboard box. He tells you where to find the street you're after, and while you're chatting, launches into a rheumy-eyed recollection of how the town once had an eccentric mayor who lived on that very street, and who imported three reindeer that he would saddle up for his triplet daughters to take rides on round the front lawn. You feel chuffed with this gem of local knowledge, and continue on to your friend's house bearing your new story as a gift.

Scene 2b. You are cruising down Main Street in a tiny country town, on the way to your friend's house. You use your car's GPS to locate the street. You drive there.

Scene 3a. You are going camping for a few days in a remote spot. You've rented a car to get there, and are borrowing a friend's Esky (an item also known as a 'cooler' or, rather charmingly, a 'chilly bin'). You see little excuse for buying one of your own, since your camping trips mostly involve hiking and eating out of a backpack. When you bring the Esky back to its owner after the trip, he gets so inspired by your description of the stunning area that he decides to make a journey there himself in a few weeks. You agree to loan him your sleeping mats for the trip, and when you stop by to drop them off, he has a house guest staying who works in a university in Montreal – which just happens to be where you're looking at applying for a job next year. He launches forth with all sorts of useful advice about the city, some of which helps you make a much better decision about how to make the move. As for the camping spot, it goes on to become one of your friend's favourite places in the world, and he forever warmly associates you with his having discovered it.

Scene 3b. You are going camping for a few days in a remote spot, and you drive down to Kmart and buy yourself an Esky to carry your spoilable food in.

BY NOT USING MONEY as the automatic solution to a need, we're compelled to depend on other humans, leading by default to a diversity of experiences. We are also incited to be both sociable humans, and fair humans, because to *not* look after our connections by being dependable and generous would leave us with a deficit of the social credit needed to get help from those around us.

Sitting in a garden may be lovely, but sitting in a garden knowing that compost you've made is helping those pumpkins grow so rambunctiously, and watching the bees pollinate the flowers that will become the apples you will eat, is a whole other magnitude of lovely. Blurring the lines between your functional and social relationships creates a similarly rich and complex feeling of being part of an ecology that you look after and that looks after you. That which we like is pleasant to us. That which we need is precious.

The truth about Epicurus

Epicurus was an ancient Greek philosopher who lived from 341 to 270 BC. For most people, his name carries with it the stink of rich cheeses, the sloshing of wine pitchers, and a general association with luxuriant gourmandising.

Records tell us that he was indeed partial to a spot of cheese, and was a great advocate for taking full pleasure in the sensual world, but in a manner far removed from the excessive indulgence suggested by his modern reputation. In fact, he firmly believed that simple meals provided as much joy as opulent ones, and saw extravagant desire as a surefire happiness-squisher: "Do not spoil what you have by desiring what you have not."

Companionship, on the other hand, he regarded as vital: "Of all the things which wisdom provides to make us entirely happy, much the greatest is the possession of friendship." Epicurus thought people should never eat alone, and should live close to a circle of friends who would nourish each other's minds, help each other in daily life, and support each other in times of struggle. He candidly described friendship as something which starts from a point of need, or from the hope of mutual benefit, but then grows into sheer pleasure at having the other person in one's life. He also viewed friendship *without* some element of mutual need as being somewhat vacuous.

Come on, look at those svelte cheekbones and tell us this wasn't a man who needed nothing more than some watered wine and barley cakes to have a good time.

Not one for merely bandying lofty ideas around, Epicurus created The Garden, a sanctuary outside Athens where those interested in studying his philosophies (including women – what would the neighbours say!) could live together by the Epicurean principles. Following his dreams obviously worked out well for him, as despite developing nasty kidney stones that made urination impossible in his old age, he apparently never complained about his suffering, and even wrote a letter to a friend on his last day on earth that described his mental state as "blissful".

31. HAVE A FINE OL' PEASANT TIME

Rural Occupations.

Coloured engraving from William Combe's A History of Madeira *(1821)*

IT WAS A BIT OF A REVELATION actually, the point at which your authors realised that sitting around doing things with our hands while talking to people felt about twice as nice as just sitting around talking to people. Even better, this handy discovery came at a bit of a low point in our journey into more concerted self-reliance.

We had begun to notice that all the food-bearing vegetation we had so excitedly surrounded our house with, and had coddled into superb health with endless loads of autumn leaves and worm castings, was making much more food than we could eat. We gave some away, swapped some, and then started trying to preserve the rest. And it took *hours*. Entire days in some cases – to strip a fruit tree, cut out any bird-peck holes, stew and bottle the whole lot. The first few sessions in a steamy kitchen, simmering tomatillos into chutney, bottling quinces, stripping branches of basil to make into pesto for freezing, and slitting olives for brining, were pleasant enough. Put on an audio book and potter away. But by the time Annie had gotten through *War and Peace* on CD, she was beginning to pine for, you know, some kind of life. With people in it.

She got really quite cynical about the joys of home food production, until a day came where she took her bushel of broad beans that needed podding with her when she popped over to have tea with her neighbour. (Young broad bean dip is delicious and freezes well: pick them when they're only fingernail-sized so they don't need double podding, lightly steam the podded beans before mashing up with olive oil, feta, lemon juice, salt and pepper.) After an hour's casual chatting, they had not only caught up on life events and worked out the details of the mulch delivery they were going to share, but all the broad beans had been podded, and no one had even noticed it happening.

What a discovery! Apricot-bottling luncheons followed! Gregarious evenings shredding old telephone books for compost while drinking apple cider and singing karaoke became a high-rotation activity! The devil may find work for idle hands to do, but from our observations, he is quite happy for it to be of the menial agricultural variety: put a pile of peas on the table to be shelled, and empty-handed company will reach out for them as eagerly as if they were a bowl of salted peanuts. Is *this* why people smoke? Need drinks to clutch at parties? A lot of us may be orally fixated, but are we manually fixated too?

Talk travels extra well when the hands are busy. Perhaps the shapes we are making with our fists and fingers help to spawn sympathetic shapes in the brain, sending thoughts off into more novel directions. Perhaps the sense that there is a background activity also narrating the space, removes just the perfect amount of pressure from conversation to allow a more luxuriant rhythm to develop. Perhaps it is the simple fact that for a fair chunk of human history, much of our conversational time must have been associated with long evenings of whittling, sewing and weaving – all the small manual tasks of DIY human culture than can be brought inside once the day has dwindled and done by fire or lamplight in a companionable fashion.

People love an activity that provides a social framework. It is one of life's most fundamental pleasures to spend time with other human beings while engaging in a challenge or accomplishing a task. Bowling alleys and boardgames; barn-raisings and beer brewing. Your authors now habitually mingle our productive time with our social time. On the smallest scale, making this happen involves keeping a stash of mending, seed-sorting, or other simple handwork within easy reach to idly work on while chatting with unexpected visitors. On the bigger scale, it involves everything from passata-making days (of the kind traditional Italian families are famed for), right through to 'nerd nights', where a group of friends hang out and investigate a topic they are all interested in.

32. PUT ON YOUR FAVOURITE POWER ANTHEM, AND BE THE ZEITGEIST

AS MUCH AS THE GREAT NOVELS of the ages celebrate outsiders; as near to our hearts as many of us clutch our anti-heroes of music and our historical rebels, ain't no one ever pretended it's easy being different. Operating somewhat to the side of the endorsed mainstream is always going to require a little fancy footwork, a little determination, and a little practice.

One struggle you may face as a frugalist in a culture of constant splurging, is good old-fashioned jealousy. Depending on your personal Achilles heel, you might find yourself gazing longingly through the shiny windows of restaurants, envying all the fancy food the people are eating. You might ogle shoes, or cars, or trendy bicycles, or thoughtlessly-consumed chocolate bars in the fists of people next to you on buses. All that stuff is nice; why the heck wouldn't you want it?

Well, let your ogling eye do a little memory trawl. Let it recall the tired, shut-down rows of faces on the train in rush hour. Let it visualise the desperate pumping of the blobby limbs spied through the gym window trying to regain some of their animal litheness. Let it observe the contrived self-consciousness of the doggedly-fashionable. Let it, if you dare, recapture the powerless anxiety in the faces of people at the last party you went to as they moved into a conversation about how hectic things are, how frustrating their job is, how tight money is right now. At about this point, you'll probably notice that you're gazing covetously again – at your own life! And that your spirit is soaring up, up, up from the ashes of jealousy, up into the phoenix-hood of glee at how much you love the way you live.

The phoenix of glee, feeling just super about tropical fruit
and tambourines, amongst other things.

Depending on what slice of society you inhabit, cutting your consumption will almost certainly disconcert a few people. They will make uncomfortable jokes when you bring coffee to work in a thermos, don't order dessert when eating out because you're already full, show up at an event pink-cheeked and windswept after riding through stormy weather to get there. Not uncommon is the technically complimentary but subtextually alienating "Omigod, you're so good…"

This soon evaporates. People are simply disconcerted by what is unfamiliar, so as you persist in your new behaviours, they will become familiar, and once again largely invisible. A few observers will generally have become curious enough along the way to ask you why you're doing what you're doing, especially when they notice you turning down overtime, losing weight, or talking about the amazing weekend you had in the mountains digging a snow cave because your tent collapsed in a storm. You explain that you're experimenting with paring back spending here and there to see if it gives you more freedom to choose what you do with life. That so far, the trade-offs seem worth it. Most people will respect this. Many will ask for tips. And the rest can go jump in a lake. It's your life, after all.

If your pre-Frugal Hedonism socialising revolved mostly around eating out, bars, and movies, it's time to seed your social life with a whole new crop of cheap thrills. Bring people wild berry picking *with* you! Invite them along to catch a train to the beach for the day. Hold a story-telling night. Play ultimate Frisbee, or chess. Take a long ramble with a friend and a dog – maybe make a date to do it weekly. Invite people round for casual dinners, lunches, breakfasts and picnics. Offer or ask someone you know for help with taking up the cuffs on a pair of pants, an IT problem, or a trombone lesson. Then eat lunch together.

Your authors will not tell a lie; we went through a teething period where we didn't replace enough of the fiscally-demanding social events we were turning down with cheaper ones. But as soon as we noted the diminished state of our social lives, we pulled our socks up, grabbed ourselves by the lapels of our secondhand jackets, and started roping friends into events like the ones listed above. People seemed to welcome our stingy catch up style with willing relief, and it hasn't been a problem since.

An incitement to a life less passive

People who step outside the box may risk being considered weird, but what if it's the whole damn culture that's gone deranged? Basic indicators of insanity would surely include traits like 'extreme loss of perspective' and 'repeatedly negating life's potential'. Using these criteria, consumer culture: *fail.* Journalist George Monbiot puts it this way:

> *Had our ancestors been asked to predict what would happen in an age of widespread prosperity in which most religious and cultural proscriptions had lost their power, how many would have guessed that our favourite activities would not be fiery political meetings, masked orgies, philosophical debates, hunting wild boar or surfing monstrous waves, but shopping and watching other people pretending to enjoy themselves? How many would have foreseen a national conversation – in public and in private – that revolves around the three R's: renovation, recipes and resorts? How many would have guessed that people possessed of unimaginable wealth and leisure and liberty would spend their time shopping for onion goggles and wheatgrass juicers? Man was born free, and he is everywhere in chainstores.*

Makes you feel pretty good about pushing the envelope a little, doesn't it?

Another aspect of frugal sociability that benefits from some determination and pizzazz are all those occasions where you are expected to bring a plate/present/wear a particular kind of outfit. Such events can find your Frugal-Hedonistically-adjusted definition of 'special' being so forcefully subsumed by that of mass culture, that you are bamboozled into rushing to the supermarket so you can arrive with yet more crackers and dips that will end up half-eaten on the table at the end of the night. Or trawling stores trying to guess what a four year-old you have never met would like for his birthday. Or forking out for a pair of shoes so unnatural to you that you will never, ever, wear them again.*

There is nothing more boring and irritating than feeling hedged into convention by these circumstances, so why not just *not* be? Presents? Only do it if you mean it and you can actually think of something that person would want. Outfits? Wear something that makes *you* feel dishy, and don't let *anyone* make you go shopping if you don't want to. Food? Luckily, so inundated have we been by mass-marketed generic products that culture is swinging back around to appreciate the idiosyncratic and the homemade. So go right ahead and bring some walnuts you pickled, a salad fresh from your garden, or some figs you heroically rescued from being obliterated by birds on that feral tree at the end of your street. *You* know how precious these things are, and you can present them to others in that light too.

Being brave enough to make up your own game plan can be hard, but it can also be a source of power. When in doubt, remind yourself why you've made the decisions you've made, and feel proud of them. Anyone worth their salt will get a kick out of your love for life. As your contentment grows in clarity, your behaviours tend to percolate into the minds and lives of those around you, and after a while, you might find that you aren't living as far from the mainstream as you had initially felt – because it has followed a few steps in your direction.

---

*   Is this shoe-demanding event a wedding, perchance? It may even be your own. If so, consider this: according to a bridal magazine study, the average 2014 spending on an Australian wedding was $65,482. That's enough to spend between six months and three years travelling together, making amazing lifelong co-memories. Or to pay for an evening's babysitting and a bottle of champagne once a week, every week, for twelve years of your marriage. We say stick up for yourselves and have a cheap one.

33. Travel cheap

IF DAILY LIFE IS STRESSFUL, having time off work and getting away from home often means one thing: doing as little as possible. You are aching to rest and recharge, and to look at beauty while you have the time to notice it. This means you crave more expensive accommodation, less challenging experiences, and idyllic surrounds.

If your daily life is not so pressured, and contains time for soaking up beauty and enjoying the elements, you are generally after contrast, interest, and adventure when you travel – all of which can be found much more cheaply.

The marvellous thing about frugal travel is the way that it compels you to get more intimate with wherever you visit. You're in a foreign land. You take the cheap local bus instead of the tourist bus, and experience the full range of ukulele buskers and tamarind candy vendors that pile aboard at every stop. Sure, the bus goes more slowly and winds around a lot, but that just gives you a chance to really absorb the scenery, or get a peek at streets you probably would never have gone down otherwise. You eat at cheap local food stalls instead of tourist restaurants. Not only do you discover a passion for sweet and sour catfish, but you get taught some regional slang that brings the house down every time you try it out.

You want to visit a national park in your state. Instead of staying in the resort and driving out to a different scenic landmark each day, you decide to do a four-day walk, camping along the way. You not only get fitter and sleep for a glorious ten hours every night, but going to bed and getting up with the sun means you get to secretly spy on animals grazing when you peep out of your tent every dawn. You bathe in secluded waterfalls that feel fantastic on your tired sweaty muscles. You notice the landscape change gradually and get excited when the soil shifts colour, or a lake appears shimmering on the horizon. At one point, you follow a small track up into a remote gorge, where you swim in the company of hundreds of iridescent dragonflies.

You've always wanted to visit France. Instead of spending three weeks hopping between tour buses and hotels, you use a house swap website and find a charming village to live in for three months. The absent owners have left you their car, and enough bicycles for your whole family to use for outings. You spend a deliriously idyllic honeymoon period acquainting yourself with all the local landmarks and gastronomic specialities, before venturing further afield to put your rapidly improving French to the test while exploring some nearby cities. When it comes time to cram a definitely-illegal quantity of camembert into your suitcases for the homeward journey, you realise that you are going have a little piece of that village stuck in your heart forever.

There are always some difficult moments in frugal travel. You will occasionally be cold/hot/lost/exhausted/eat something unidentifiable. But these are often the bits that make you realise that you're tougher than you thought. *And* the bits that make the best stories. Besides, people who take a trip expecting everything to be glitch-free and cushy often get more annoyed by a lukewarm meal than a frugal traveller does by taking a bus five hours in the wrong direction. Perhaps most importantly of all, while pricier travel does buy a higher base level of 'pleasantness', it seldom provides moments of euphoria or revelation as generously as frugal travel does.

Perhaps not surprisingly, the Frugal Hedonist is rather permissive when defining 'travel'. Your authors think that travel is ultimately about creating a contrast with everyday life, thereby refreshing your mind and making time seem more spacious.

Last summer the two of us 'travelled' for a mere twelve hours. We decided to walk all night long, aiming to reach a semi-rural train station on the farthest fringe of the city. We selected a date with a full moon and clear skies, and took a long afternoon nap with an alarm clock set for sunset. Then after downing some strong coffee and throwing some sandwiches into a bag, we started walking. We were repeatedly captivated and distracted by small details while passing through neighbourhoods we had never seen before – a surreal tableau in a backlit window, a giant topiary mouse in an otherwise conventional garden, completely nonsensical signage on a souvlaki shop, an intoxicating floral scent that had us sniffing after it up alleyways until we located the source. We watched the streets segue from dense inner-urban studded with honking cars, greasy spoon eateries and the sound of drum solos tumbling out of bars, to stately suburban with huge fragrant lawns, to identical kit homes, to light industrial, to ramshackle cottages dotted between small fields full of sleeping horses. We marched along the deserted moonlit train tracks singing, jumped when sudden kangaroos bounded across our path, paddled our aching feet in the cool dark silk of 3am streams. We arrived at the final train station on the line just as the stars started to evaporate, and let the first train of the day whisk us back to the city.

This adventure was fascinating, enjoyable, and nearly free – $3.20 each for our train tickets home. We felt like we'd been away for days by the time we got back home. It also gave us 40km worth of leg exercise, and made life seem more magnificent and full of infinite potential for weeks afterwards.

Slightly further afield, your authors have developed an autumn tradition of camping at the edge of a desert park. We can hitchhike or take a train to the park's closest town, walk for 10km and find ourselves in the middle of a quiet, hot landscape of small brittle plants, jewelled insects, and a slow lazy river to swim in. We walk barefoot in the burning sand a lot, sleep even more, read stories, eat little. Once our backpacks are empty of the food we brought, we fill them with wild olives from the trees that are the bane of the local park rangers' existence, and walk out again. We feel ridiculously rejuvenated, and have our year's supply of olives to boot.

Not all forms of frugal travel will suit everyone. Know what your basic requirements for staying happy and healthy are, and choose travel configurations that will meet them. For example, we have a travelling friend who eats anything and will happily bed down on any sort of ground, but needs quiet to sleep well. She has surprised her work-exchange hosts by offering to sleep in her tent rather than in a cosy (but noisy) room in the house, and has sought out couchsurfing hosts who are retired geology professors rather than nightlife aficionados of her own age. The key is to find styles of travel that work with both your loves and your limits. For websites that might help you discover what those are, see our Further Resources section.

Hint: don't use a camera too much, they get in between your eyeballs and this feeling.

34. LIBERATE YOURSELF FROM THE TERROR OF GRIME

COSMETIC AND DETERGENT COMPANIES would have us believe that if we don't use large globs of their products on a frequent basis, our friends will all desert us, and we'll develop a host of communicable diseases. Your authors suspect that they may be keeping their profit margins – rather than our best interests – at heart when doling out advice.

By the time we're teenagers, most of us are convinced that a legion of body washes, facial wipes, pantyliners, skin serums, foot deodorisers and mouth gargles* are required to prevent ourselves from becoming repellent. Then there's protecting ourselves from our hideous homes with kitchen wipes,

---

* So you've probably noticed by now that we harbour an inappropriate love of footnotes, but we think you'll cut us some slack over this one, because it really is a gem: a lot of those 'germs' that hygiene product advertisements love to warn us about are actually essential to human health and happiness! We have symbiotically evolved with these little guys helping to do all sorts of jobs around our body that our own cells aren't that good at. And there are really a lot of them on the job. Our skin contains around 50 million bacteria per square inch. There are ten times more bacteria cells in our digestive tract than we have human cells in our body – in a healthy person anyway. Evidence suggests that pleasant breath and body odour, skin health, maintaining a healthy weight, immune system function and digestive health are all improved by encouraging a healthy diversity of bodily bacteria. Insufficient bacterial diversity may even contribute to anxiety and autism spectrum disorders.

surface sprays, grout bleaches and air fresheners. Folks, it's all a big swindle. Even basics like soap, laundry detergent and dishwashing liquid can generally be used at one quarter the suggested rate to exactly the same effect, and all the other stuff is pretty much unnecessary.

If you work in an office and take a bus to work, you probably don't need to wash your clothes after a day's wear. Heck, it's unlikely that you need to wash *yourself* after a day's wear, especially if you're pretty healthy via your Frugal Hedonistic living. Don't get us wrong here, we don't like having the funk any more than the next guy, but we've experimented a bit and found that being clean just isn't that complex.

Cowboys supposedly believed that washing too much could sap your vitality. Actually, we suspect we gleaned this 'fact' from some long-forgotten matinee movie, but funnily enough modern research is beginning to back the superstition up. Read the footnote!

So fresh and so clean

Most people are wise to the wonders of bicarbonate soda and white vinegar for household cleaning, but here are a few other frugal home hygiene tips that might not have made it onto your radar yet:

~ Hanging clothes out on a sunny or breezy day instead of washing them. (For clothes that don't have actual muck on them, but just need a bit of freshening). We have a vague idea that a granny once told us this was called 'sunwashing', which sounds a bit magical as a bonus.

~ Using newspaper to clean windows and mirrors. Start with a scrunched couple of sheets, dunk them in a bucket of water, and use them to do a good rubbing. Then get a sheet or two of dry stuff to work over the windows in a polishing motion. They get really shiny. It's something in the ink apparently.

~ Ash. If you produce any in your household, it makes a great cleaning agent anywhere there is grease, like a roasting dish, an oven, or post-washing-up sink. Just scoop up some of the finer stuff into a container, dip a wet scrubber into it, and scrub-a-dub. We know it sounds odd, but it's actually a traditional use of ash, plus it works.

~ Having a rag bag. Paper towels are crazy-business. Cut the fabric up into squares for ease of use, and toss them or wash them after use, as you please. Old towels, sheets or cotton shirts are perfect.

~ Putting on loud music and really throwing yourself into the elbow grease and exercise factor.

~ Embracing Tom Hodgkinson's advice from his book *How to Be Free*: "If you want a cleaner house, simply turn off the lights and fire up a candle. Electric light is the enemy." He also suggests avoiding pale bed linens unless you have a staff of servants, and eschewing white or laminate-coated furniture in favour of wood. Now that's a clever chap.

35. And a wee tiny comment on condiments

You can buy things marinated in oil and vinegar. You can also buy flavoured oils and vinegars. Ridiculous to do both! Keep the vinegar from that jar of capers or the oil from that jar of marinated whatever, and use it for cooking. If it makes you happier about it, pour it into a fresh jar and label it 'caper-infused white wine vinegar'.

In general however, the frugal gourmand limits the buying of expensive pre-mixed products in the first place. Especially all those ones that just combine three things you had in the cupboard anyway to make a dukkah, cajun spice mix or stir-fry sauce, or where they put some stuff in oil with a few sprigs of herbs and a chilli. "Why, I could do that in my sleep!" you declare upon closer inspection, and you feel the shackles of culinary slavery melting away.

Even better, if you acquire enough Frugal Hedonist friends, at least a couple of them will have home-preserving inclinations, and will be proudly pushing jars of pickles and pesto upon you willy-nilly. And chutney. Be prepared for a wealth of chutney.

36. UNDERCOMPLI-CATE THINGS

OVER THE YEARS, your authors have become wise to a couple of specific consumption genres that can lure a Frugal Hedonist in. They do this by their very aura of being investments in a longer-term good life. If you are a reformed big-spender who is transitioning to Frugal Hedonism: alert! You are particularly at risk of accidentally replacing your previous consumption habits with new ones, and the following three categories are prime contenders.

Eco-tech products

Surely it is justifiable – nay, even noble – to spend your hard-earned money on a new water-efficient washing machine. Or a set of bamboo fibre sheets, or a hybrid car. But while these purchases may carry the bonus of supporting worthwhile new products and industries, don't kid yourself that they are your most resource-frugal option. The greenest product you're ever going to get, is almost always *the one that you (or somebody else) already have*. The energy costs that go into making and distributing even energy-efficient, sustain-ably-sourced new objects is very high. Generally much higher than whatever energy you will save by using that object rather than continuing to maintain and use an old object until it is truly worn out.

Mini-example? The guy who buys a fully-biodegradable plant-gum-based waterproof sheath to protect his phone when he goes fishing is being *less* green than if he had just wrapped it in an old plastic bag. Mega-example?

The couple that pour all their money into building a brand new eco-home, complete with non-toxic paints, passive solar design and state-of-the-art composting toilet are being *less* green than if they had just kept caring for and living in the old cottage that was on the land when they bought it.

So before hitting the eco-product catalogues, explore your other resource-frugal options! The gold class response is to change your behaviour so as to **avoid or reduce the need to consume** in the first place. Next on the ladder comes identifying a **low-tech solution**, or **using an object that already exists**.

Let's use that couple in their old cottage to illustrate. They don't install solar panels, but they do install a second-hand skylight in the main living space so that they don't need to use the lights as much (low-tech, pre-existing object). They don't even rip out the old gas heater to put in a new slow combustion one, but they scarcely use it, because they fill in all the drafty chinks around the doors and windows, and use all the tricks mentioned in tip "44. Acclimatise to the seasons" to stay warm and cool (pre-existing object, low-tech, behavioural). They also save energy in myriad small ways: only boiling as much water as they need when making hot drinks, using lids on cooking pots, and turning the oven/stove burners off early so food finishes cooking via residual heat (all behavioural). The beauty of such solutions is that not only are they the most resource frugal, they're also usually the most financially frugal.

Self-sufficiency accessories

If part of your vision for your Frugal Hedonism makeover includes doing a fair bit of home food production, this one's for you. In all the rampant excitement of contemplating your new way of life, you might feel inclined to go hog-wild buying accessories to 'help you do it properly'. Preserving kits, grain mills, dehydrators, specialised gardening tools, ice cream/yoghurt/bread makers, sprouters, fermentation crocks, seed-raising igloos; the potential for spending is endless. Several of these products are really great to use, and some of them even help do the job more safely (e.g., home preserving kits do make it easier to sterilise your jars). None of them are particularly necessary however.

HRH Prince Charles in 2007 test drives a Saab BioPower convertible which runs on up to 85% ethanol. A few months earlier, the Earth Policy Institute had reported that, "The grain required to fill a 25-gallon fuel tank of a sport utility vehicle with ethanol just once would feed one person for a whole year." Lesson: it is rare to find any real alternative to simply consuming less.

There is an irony too, about buying stuff to help you with not buying stuff. Much more fun in general is to equip yourself with the knowledge to let you do it using things you already have. Before embarking on a new project, do a little research to acquaint yourself with the underlying principles, then apply that knowledge to your sauerkraut-making or seed-raising or whatever it is. Knowledge is *true* self-sufficiency. Old jars are a great help.

That way, if you discover that you're not that into making sauerkraut after all, there is no great loss. Alternatively, if you discover that you love bottling tomatoes and you've done it in jars sterilised in the oven for three years running, and have maybe even borrowed a friend's preserving kit for a test drive, then buying a second hand kit online could be a great decision.

Superfoods

You might feel like handing over chunky money for coconut water, vitamins, spirulina power bars, and goji berry powder is a worthwhile exception to your frugal ways; an investment in your health. You're probably wrong. Don't forget that the distributors of health food products are companies too, who often work very hard to create a lot of media spin around some very small, cherry-picked studies. If you have specific deficiencies that need fixing, maybe go there. Apart from that, most of us would probably do better by simply eating a diversity of fresh, whole foods with utmost relish, while not overeating, moving a lot, and having a really good time.

37. Figure out what you really *do* enjoy spending money on

Ice cream, ice cream, travel, ice cream, whiskey, ice cream. Ice cream. But each to their own. Across-the-board frugality is a deeply satisfying challenge for some personality types, but for many readers of this book, giving your consumption habits a good, hard eyeballing will lead to more of a thoughtful tweaking here, a painless paring there, and an unabashed prioritising right in the sweet spot.

Would you like your authors to use ridiculous pseudonyms to discuss a couple of our own friends by way of example? Happy to oblige.

> **Rufous Scrub and Jean Door** both work part time. They do jobs that, although not their dream jobs, are in their chosen fields. They don't take many holidays, possibly because they aren't overworked, and very much enjoy books, vigorous conversation, and staying at home and drinking wine in the garden. Sometimes in a paddling pool. While playing darts.

> They probably wouldn't nominate themselves as particularly frugal, but they have chosen to evolve life habits that minimize their costs and maximize their pleasures, rather than working more. They are very computer-adept, and save money by sourcing a lot of books, movies etc. cheaply online. They also get a kick out of using their skills to fix and

improve their computers, audio gear, phones, and anything electrical around the house. They build some of their technology out of components, allowing a better standard of equipment for less money.

They have similar skills with bicycles, which they use to go everywhere, and maintain in good condition. They have no car. They buy minimal clothes and home accessories, valuing scavenged furniture and simple, stylish clothing.

They are passionate about food and drink, and have a small but intensely productive vegetable garden to provide better quality fresh ingredients. They preserve a few things like lemons and onions, not to save money, but so that they can have the best pickled onions and preserved lemons – though save them money it does. They brew their own beer because they love figuring out how to make excellent beer, and so that they can be generous with it when friends appear.

They also buy in bulk stuff they use a lot of, like good anchovies or olives. In some cases they split a bulk buy of something like olive oil with other foodie friends, saving them all money and packaging while getting a better product.

They don't skimp on the things that make them really happy. Eating out at amazing venues, classy gin, the most decadent cheese. Nor on those things that both make them happy, *and* make their lives more functional, like parts for their bikes or computers, cooking equipment, or music.

THESE FINE CATS are just one example of the very modern concept of 'pick-n-mix' frugality that we suspect would not just work nicely, but be a relief for many people who are exhausting themselves trying to 'have it all'.

Having it all probably isn't as great as it's cracked-up to be anyway. There is something inarguably dull about striving to tick every box considered appropriate for your approximate social demographic. And at the extreme end of the got-it-all spectrum, have you heard about the therapy bills those 'enviable' types with designer lounge suites and private pilates instructors are racking up? Choose patchy purchasing for mental and fiscal health today!!!

And the prize for the most enjoyable use of money goes to...

Experiences. Research is now backing up what most philosophers have been hinting at since the year dot: experiences are a better investment than stuff.

An overview of data from across the social sciences has found that once basic needs have been met, "increases in our stocks of material goods produce virtually no measurable gains in our psychological or physical well-being", despite our expectations to the contrary. Experiences, on the other hand, really deliver. So why don't we think of them as a good investment? Possibly because the memories, pleasure, human camaraderie and learning that they bestow lack an easily measureable dollar value.

James Wallman, author of *Stuffication*, has come up with five big factors that help explain why experiences win:

1. The hedonic treadmill. This is the process of getting used to, or even bored of, material acquisitions we once coveted, so that we constantly need new acquisitions to maintain the same level of happiness. It doesn't happen with the memories or expanded sense of self that we gain from significant experiences.

2. Positive reinterpretation. When we buy an unsatisfactory material product, we tend just to feel pissed off. When an experience goes wrong, it can often be as worthwhile as when it goes right. Think of that time that you journeyed to the beach for a nice day of swimming, but forgot your bathers. You mustered the courage to swim in your underwear, and then did mad Olympic sprints between the ocean and your towel in the hope that no one would notice what you were wearing. The friend who came with you laughed at you all day long, you laughed when you related the story to people that evening, they laughed to hear about it, and you felt a little bit braver to boot. This effect can be found even with experiences that were quite gruelling at the time, as was noted by Seneca (the ancient Roman philosopher) when he said, "Things that were hard to bear are sweet to remember."

3. Comparability. It's much harder to compare experiences than it is material goods. And hence harder to be insecure about whether the one *you* had measures up.

4. Experiences create identity. Training for and competing in a marathon, learning how to make perfect crêpes, having a weekly poker night with friends, eating fermented shark meat while in Iceland, or volunteering at an animal shelter all become part of our story of self. Much more than a new hall rug ever could – easier to transport too. Plus, anyone sane would rather hear you talk about any of the above than receive a sermon on the great new venetian blinds you've just had installed.

5. Social connection. Experiences tend to bring us closer to people in a way that purchases simply can't. And strong human connections are a better indicator of health and happiness than any other single factor.

38. FREE UP YOUR FRIVOLITY

THE DESIRE TO BUY unnecessary things is very strong – it can feel like an assertion of freedom from the parade of functional activities that constitute much of life; like leisure and light-heartedness in the face of too much work and worry. This kind of purchasing certainly *can* result in something that will be enjoyed, but often it is simply a flawed attempt to create a new life ratio of frivolity vs. functionality. Or to add 'value' to life by getting things that have a cost and hence the inherent *implication* of value.

Ironically, many of these pleasure-purchases actually result in a later need for even more functional activity. It might be cupboards and drawers that require endless cleaning out because they are overflowing with unworn clothes which need sorting/folding/washing/mending/taking to the charity donation bin; the extra jiggle on the belly that seems to demand an increased gym regime; the bigger house that needs more cleaning and repairs. On the most basic level, it might just be the credit card bill that needs you to do more overtime to pay it off.

Living light-heartedly is an altogether different beast. It involves being a bit philosophical about bad things that happen, so that they don't dominate your mind or outlook. Or retaining the ability to take delight in fleeting moments. Or recognizing that being frivolous, spontaneous or playful with other humans and within your own head is a totally free present you can give to yourself and the people around you as often as you like. This stuff is the *real* assertion of freedom from the drabber elements of daily life: don't get it confused with frivolous spending.

*Life is short. So why not channel your longing for a life less-ordinary
and more spontaneous into footwear purchases?*

39. LIMIT THE BURDEN OF CHOICE

ONE LONG RAINY DAY, your author Annie decided it was a perfect movie-watching type of afternoon, so she scampered through the downpour and knocked on her neighbour's front door. She knew this neighbour to be the possessor of hundreds of cinematic titles, and thought there'd surely be something in his collection to tickle her fancy. As she scanned the seemingly endless options, she started to feel kind of flustered, and also less and less excited by watching any of them. After a ridiculous amount of time, she left having borrowed four movies that looked pretty good. She watched between twelve and twenty minutes of each, deciding in every case that she wasn't really into it, but maybe the next one would be what she was after. She felt somehow like a failure, both for finding it so hard to choose, and for not being able to enjoy any of her choices. She remembered thoroughly enjoying random second-rate movies she'd encountered on long-haul buses, and while owning a TV with only one channel. What had changed? She thought about going back next door to see if there was anything else there that might be what she was *really* after, but felt irrational irritation at her lovely neighbour for having such an immense movie collection. The whole exercise had been a bit wearying anyway. She cuddled the dog and had a snooze instead.

Does the essence of this tale feel familiar? Perhaps you'll recognize something in the following situations too: You're standing on the street corner trying to decide on a dining option. Do you feel more like Thai, pizza or Lebanese?

Thai is closest, pizza is cheaper, Lebanese seems somehow healthier. Distress is mounting, you're having a strangely tense conversation with your Significant Other about the relative merits of what to have for dinner… Now imagine you're drifting off to sleep after spending the evening reading an evocative Danish novel about a lonely aesthete astronomer. You're pretty sure you should be having meandering poetical thoughts about our smallness in the face of the stars or something, but instead you're wondering about those new shoes you bought today. Should you have gotten the slightly chunkier ones? Will that toe shape even work with any of your pants? Should you have gone for black after all? Black would have been more versatile, but you loved that stitching detail on the brown…

A little choice is very nice. A large range of choices encourages perennial dissatisfaction with whatever you have chosen, no matter how satisfactory it is – you might not have picked the best option, after all! According to Barry Schwartz, psychologist and author of the *Paradox of Choice,* when choice abounds, we feel that if things don't turn out so great it is because *we* made poor decisions, not because there just weren't any great options available. Hence the 'luxury' of choice often comes with a sense of pressure around making the *right* one, which can lead to anxiety and regret. To top it all off, research has shown that the process of attempting to constantly evaluate and decide between options – as we do all day long in affluent societies – creates serious mental fatigue. (Post-lunch slump? Maybe it's *not* the carbs. You just need to switch to a sandwich bar with fewer potential combinations of drink + bread-variety + filling!)

The fantastic news for Frugal Hedonists is that by consuming less, the range of consumer decisions you have to confront on a daily basis plummets. If you always make your own salad dressing, you'll never find yourself in the supermarket gazing bleakly at the 93 varieties on the shelf. If you basically only buy secondhand, and take pleasure in taking your luck where it comes, you'll never find yourself standing in the Ikea checkout line in tormented indecision about whether to sprint back and swap that set of towels for the darker blue ones before it is too late. If you usually put together your bicycles out of salvaged parts, you'll never have to deliberate whether a retro cruiser or an Italian road bike would better reflect your personal style. If you have

List of 403(b) Certified Companies as of July 11, 2014				
Name of Certified Company	**Annuity**	**Non-Annuity**	**TRS #**	**Phone Number**
AXA Equitable Life Insurance Company	x		12-047-01	800-628-6673
Allianz Global Investors Distributors, LLC		x	11-102-02	800-988-8380
American Century Investments		x	10-080-02	800-345-3533
American Funds Distributors, Inc.		x	12-011-02	800-421-9900
American United Life Insurance Company	x		12-062-01	800-249-6269
Americo Financial Life and Annuity	x		12-053-01	800-231-0801
Annuity Investors Life Insurance Company	x		12-003-01	800-438-3398
Athene USA	x		12-016-01	800-800-9882
BlackRock, Inc.		x	12-105-02	212-810-5300
CLS Investments, LLC		x	14-107-02	402-493-3313
Columbia Management Investment		x	12-048-02	800-345-6611
Commonwealth Annuity and Life Co.	x		13-090-01	800-457-9047
Deutsche Asset & Wealth Management		x	13-066-02	800-728-3337
Dimensional Funds		x	12-104-02	866-300-5943
Federated Funds		x	11-083-02	888-367-3777
Fidelity Investments		x	12-012-02	800-343-08W60
Fidelity Security Life Insurance Company	x		12-051-01	800-648-8624
First Investors Corporation		x	12-008-02	800-423-4026
Franklin Templeton Investments		x	13-054-02	800-530-2432
GWN Securities, Inc.			10-101-04	561-472-2700
Great American Insurance Group	x		13-089-01	800-438-3398
Great-West Life and Annuity Insurance	x	x	12-071-03	866-467-7756
Guggenheim Investments		x	14-093-02	800-820-0888
Hartford Life Insurance Company	x		12-056-01	800-528-9009
Horace Mann	x		12-027-01	800-999-1030
ING Life Insurance and Annuity Company	x		12-032-01	800-262-3862
Invesco Distributors, Inc		x	12-012-02	800-959-4246
ISC Group, Inc.	x		12-104-02	800-888-3520

It's not just you; most people's eyes glaze over when looking at lists like this. A study found that for every 10 additional retirement funds workers are given to choose from, a further 2% of people give up on making a choice at all. Other studies have shown that when you give people over 10 options they make poorer decisions, even in critical areas such as health insurance and investments.

already decided that your current bathroom is totally adequate, you'll never find yourself trawling online shower screen catalogues for six hours straight in search of the Perfect One.

And that's not a bad thing. Seeking the perfect choice, says Schwartz, even in big decisions like colleges, "is a recipe for misery". Research indicates that those of us who tend to put a lot of effort and research into our choices, actually get less pleasure per dollar, and are less content overall – despite usually managing to select a slightly superior option. This could be partly because we become inclined to *expect* perfection after a lot of careful weighing-up of pros and cons, and yet perfection is always a concept, never a reality. But while this effect is exaggerated for the ultra-thorough consumer, it applies to choice-rich societies in general; with so much available we develop a delusion that we should always be able to get what we want, and feel ripped off and depressed when we don't.

The Frugal Hedonist does not expect perfection. The Frugal Hedonist expects that life will be a multi-coloured journey of pleasures and struggles and joy and death and adventure and boredom and epiphany and love and loss and getting drenched in storms and dry by fires and sometimes eating slightly stale bread but not minding and sometimes eating freshly plucked raspberries and being jubilant. He regards most shops and restaurants as giant lumps in the landscape, to save himself from adding more candidates to his ballot paper of potential consumables. She recognizes that although endless choice promises endless freedom, it also entraps us in an endless series of fine-tuned decisions that we feel must be well-made to encourage success and accurately reflect our identity. So, she makes some broad decisions to spare her brain this gruelling banality.

Such broad decisions can be big or small. We know a family who decided years ago to never shop in a supermarket again. Most of our friends wouldn't think to buy bottled water – it's not some ongoing act of piety, they've just taken it off their radar as a way to get water. Some people identify a small handful of body and cleaning products that suit them, and do away with keeping an eye out for other options. Others have a 'no-phones no-computers after 6pm' rule (with the aim of removing the ongoing choice of whether to squeeze in a little bit more work or not). Personally, your authors find it hard to pin down our own blanket decisions, for even though they must have been somewhat conscious at some stage, the whole point is that they just morph into habit over time, making them totally normal and effortless. We don't buy magazines or newspapers, or get takeaway coffees, or take taxis (unless it's an emergency), or visit hair salons. It just wouldn't occur to us to buy stuff like pre-mixed pancake batter, or hand-freshening towelettes, or yoghurt in tubes, or air deodoriser, or eggs or meat with a depressing past, or big bags of chips with lots of little bags of chips inside.

Once your simple rules of engagement become second nature, they don't usually require strict adherence. For example, your authors wouldn't normally buy fast food from a mega-franchise, but have done it twice in the last five years. Once, because it seemed like the most perverse thing we could do immediately upon completing a book about foraging, and once because we were stuck by a highway with no other options. We felt fine about these exceptions – there's no obligation to be dogmatic about avoiding consumer options that you've decided you're better off without. The point is to not have them cluttering up your brain on a daily basis, clamouring to be assessed for relative desirability and merit. Imagine a time where you just got milk in a bottle that said 'milk', and you didn't have to think about milk any more than that. That's what we're sort of faking here. Relaxing, isn't it?

40. DON'T BE A SNOOTY BUM BUM

THE TITLE OF THIS TIP is embarrassingly uncultivated. And yet not unlovable. Which is in fact the point.

One result of the endless variety of consumables now available is that we tend to hone in on the subtlest minutiae of delineation between – what would appear to a caveperson to be – nearly identical products. Whether it's Coke vs. Pepsi, or slightly varied cuts of jeans, it's our ability to see the difference that defines us as a Person of Taste. But it can sure get in the way of knowing what it is we *actually* like.

When it comes to being discerning about food and drink, there's good evidence that we kid ourselves when we think we can distinguish between similar flavours. For instance, in 2011, British Professor Richard Wiseman (a former stage magician) arranged for 578 people to taste wines ranging from a £3.78 claret to a £30 champagne. When the participants were asked to guess if a particular wine cost less than £5 or more than £10, their answers were no more accurate than if they'd flipped a coin! Embarrassingly, professional wine tasters don't fare much better. In one French study, all 54 wine experts failed to notice that they were tasting two identical white wines – except that one had been dyed red with a tasteless dye. They described the white using terms like 'honey', 'lychee' and 'straw', and the dyed red wine with words like 'coal', 'raspberry' and 'clove'. Our evaluation of flavour also shifts in response to hunger, room temperature, music, our moods and activities. And, of course, cultural values…

Thirty years ago legions of people who now recoil in horror at anything but a perfect espresso were completely capable of enjoying a cup of instant coffee. Iceberg lettuce was a legitimate occupant of a salad bowl, whereas now only heathens (or, confusingly, those within the cutting-edge retro-food movement) are found enjoying its glacial crunch.

The whole idea of 'superior' taste sensations is a tad shaky anyway, since our sensitivity to odours and flavours – and whether we find them pleasant or not – varies widely from person to person. Each of us has about 400 odour receptors, but pretty much no two people outside of identical twins share the same combination of them. So maybe if you're still a closet-drinker of instant coffee you are really just more receptive to its finer flavours than some other people. Either that or you have an admirable capacity to enjoy the less-than-perfect. Who can say? Certainly no one but you!

We once chatted with a young lady who'd spent a long stretch of time co-housing with people with Down's syndrome. She told us that when she left, she found it stultifying how much time and energy her friends invested in putting things through a filter of how Cool or Right they were before being able to enjoy them. The Down's syndrome people had simply liked whatever made them happy, regardless of cultural cringe-abilty.

Adam remembers getting a hitchhike with a guy who'd had a brain tumour removed and been left with a freakishly powerful sense of smell. He drove Adam all the way home, and accepted the offer of a bunch of fresh coriander from the herb garden in the front yard. Deeply inhaling the smell of the coriander caused him to cackle with unadulterated delight, and when invited in, he displayed immense enjoyment in smelling everything from the pepper grinder to the wood of the cupboard doors. Unusual behaviour in a guest, but definitely a man whom no one could tell what to take pleasure in, nor how to carefully moderate his opinions of things and behave with only appropriate levels of appreciation.

Okay. There are of course many cases where quality really does count towards enjoyability. Your authors simply wouldn't bother eating cheap waxy chocolate, because we don't think it tastes any good at all. But frequently the difference between those things that are out of favour with the tastemakers and those that they are applauding is inanely subtle, and we'd do well to just go with our guts. The Frugal Hedonist is a master of the art of enjoying, and you can enjoy anything you damn well enjoy enjoying! You don't need to have The Best, because The Best probably isn't inherently the best anyway. And even if it really, really seems like it is, it won't by next year.

But if you're still struggling to shun your addiction to being a Person of Taste, try this argument from Selwyn H. Pendercrast*:

> *Any idiot can appreciate the quality of something good. Only the true connoisseur can perfectly distinguish the fine and noble flavours amongst those dank and sulphurous. So that's why I bought the cheap bottle.*

---

* Your authors readily confess this man to be an entirely made-up character. We just wanted to attribute our own quote to someone with a much fancier name.

41. SELF-PROPEL

SURE THAT DIAL ON THE SPEEDOMETER goes up to a tantalising
240 kilometres (150 miles) an hour. But how fast does your car really go,
on average? We're not alluding merely to time stuck in traffic here. To truly
calculate the 'effective speed' of our vehicles we need to include all the hours
we put in at the office to cover fuel, registration and other running costs…
with that speedometer sitting right on zero all the while. One Australian
study calculates that for every hour spent driving a Toyota Landcruiser, the
average owner spends another 1.5 hours working to pay for it. The study also
points out that if the owner had to pay for their car's 'externalities' – those
costs borne by society – of CO_2 emissions, traffic congestion and the cost of
road accidents, they'd need to work another 0.6 hours for every hour behind
the wheel. That puts the effective speed of a Landcruiser at 9 kilometres (5.7
miles) per hour. Not so convenient after all, eh? A bicycle, by the way, with
its far lower purchase, running, and externality costs, clocks in at a relatively
speedy 18 kilometres (11 miles) per hour.

In Australia, the annual registration, running and depreciation costs of a mid-
range newish car are around $12,000 per year. And that's excluding all those
parking tickets. Let's be generous and estimate that in the case of an older car,
lower depreciation costs could knock that figure right down to $7,000. Even
for this bottom-end figure you could take three $20 taxi rides every week, *and*
pay for a rental car plus a hundred dollars worth of petrol for fourteen weekends per year, and still come out ahead. By way of further comparison, Adam's
total transport costs in the year of writing this were $610, which included a
major bicycle service, weekly public transport, and multiple train trips to the
country. So even if you add a bit of depreciation on the bike, there's still a
handy bit of pocket change left out of our hypothetical seven grand.

Some folks we know, Paul and Nikki, have worked out another transport configuration. They didn't like being forced to use their car when they wanted to take their kids places, so they bought a 'cargo' bike – like a grownup tricycle with a tray in the front deep enough for a couple of toddlers or a mega-load of shopping. It worked so well that they *almost* got rid of their car. But they still wanted it for occasional trips. So instead, they use a network called Car Next Door to share their car with the neighbours. Car sharing is a rapidly growing business. The biggest network in the US is Zipcar, and co-founder Robin Chase says, "Each Zipcar replaces 15 personal cars. And each driver drives about 80% less because they're now paying the full cost all at once in real time." So when Paul was asked by his council to enter a 'design your dream streetscape' competition, he found himself calculating that if all his street's residents joined share-car networks, they would only use about six cars between them: "Our street is 200 metres by 8 metres. That's 1,600 square metres of space. … So my dream makeover? Dig the whole road up except for two five-space car parks at each end that hold share cars and some visitor parking. By my reckoning that would enable the planting of 150-odd fruit and nut trees

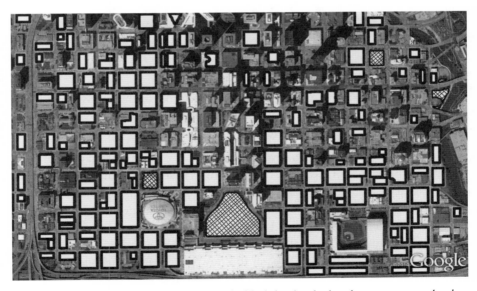

Parking lots and parks in Houston, Texas. The black-bordered white boxes are vacant land or parking lots. The cross-hatched areas are parks (the kind with trees and grass).

Cars need a lot of space: three people travelling by car
(assuming single occupancy) vs. three people travelling by bicycle.

plus companion planting, which should provide most of the [perishable] food
for the street." If car sharing continues on its current trajectory, these kinds of
visions might soon be sounding very sane.

It may be impossible to do what you currently do, and where you currently do
it, without heavy use of a car. Morning routines that involve dropping kids off,
collecting dry cleaning, then crossing town to get to work, often can't be done
by public transport or bike. But then, major savings, like getting rid of a car
(or switching to a smaller one and using it half as much), sometimes require
major life reshaping. It is usually worth it. You will be astonished by how
much more money you have. You get to know your neighbourhood better,
because you walk down the streets rather than pulling out of the driveway
in a bubble. You can gaze dreamily out the window on a train. You can also

read books (not so good while driving) and witness heartwarming scenes, like teenage goths helping old ladies wrestle their walking frames in through the doors. You're more focussed and take fewer sick days at school or work if you walk or ride to get there.* Going car-free does mean planning errands in blocks, and on really rainy nights you might settle for cranking up the Michael Jackson for a boogie in your living room instead of cycling to that Zumba class two suburbs away, but then you probably don't need to do either, what with all the exercise you've been getting while walking and riding about so much.

Choosing where you live and what you do as though car travel didn't exist, tends to have instant money-saving effects in other areas too. Living in a smaller home so that you can be close to amenities and public transport saves you money and time in heating, cleaning and furnishings (and in home maintenance and possibly loan repayments if you own your own home). Doing fewer shopping trips per week saves you money on impulse buys. Deciding to work from home all or part of the week saves money on takeaway lunches and coffees. Riding to and from work, instead of spending money on petrol to drive to a gym where you pay to ride on a stationary bicycle is not only much cheaper, but infinitely less absurd. The only thing you might spend more money on is extra cream to pour over your apple crumble of an evening, because boy does self-propulsion make you *hungry*!

Time for a recap. A bit of number crunching reveals that cars don't actually save you time. For those on a modest income, the choice to run a car or not can make the difference between feeling permanently financially stretched... and sailing smoothly through each pay period. This difference is something worth rearranging your life for. Riding, walking and using public transport keep you socially connected and in spiffing shape. What's more, cars make everything smell bad, and have enabled the rise and rise of horrible big-box architecture and land-hungry suburban sprawl.

All this said, your authors actually think cars are amazing machines, so long as they are treated as the use-only-when-needed objects that anything so socially,

---

*   A 2013 U.K. study found that people who cycled to work took an average of half as many sick days as those who drove. A Danish study showed that children who came to school by car, bus or train performed worse on concentration tests than those who walked or rode.

environmentally and personally costly should be. If you *do* decide you have to keep one, try using this simple test for whether to use it: imagining there was only a pool of rentable vehicles, would you go to the effort and expense of hiring one for the occasion in question, or would you come up with an alternative? Driving ten blocks to the supermarket because you forgot to get orange juice when you were there yesterday would literally *never* pass this test.

In praise of walking

"Walking ... is how the body measures itself against the earth."
~ Rebecca Solnit, *Wanderlust: A History of Walking*

One of your authors' favourite things about not having a car is how you come to regard your legs as having serious transportation capacity. Humans used to hunt antelope by *running them down*, for crying out loud! We knew a man who spent some time teaching agricultural workshops in Peru, and he described how grandmothers would show up for class in this mountainous location, having thought nothing of taking a three day walk to get there.

We are made to move, and both body and mind seem to thrive on the gentle, rhythmic motion that is walking. Kinks in your body sort themselves out. Your brain's problem-solving and creative capacities seem heightened while walking. There's a wonderful feeling to be gotten simply by using your feet to carry you somewhere you'd normally take a bus to. It may take a couple of hours, but you'll arrive enlivened and mentally refreshed, plus you'll relate to that journey differently ever after.

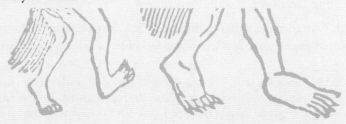

42. Have less house

ADMITTEDLY HE'S AN ESCAPED BANK ROBBER rather than an expert on human happiness, but Gregory David Roberts' words "I sometimes think that the size of our happiness is inversely proportional to the size of our house" are worth pondering. (He wrote them in his quasi-autobiographical novel, *Shantaram*, in response to living for several years in the slums of Mumbai.)

If you've ever lived in a tent for an extended time, you'll probably agree that having *no* stable domestic space has some downsides. You can spend a lot of time each day reshuffling objects to enable cooking, washing, dressing and sleeping. Just having a shelf to keep your muesli on can seem pretty darn nifty after having spent months re-submerging it in your backpack after each use. Also fantastic is somewhere undercover to hang clothes to dry, and some space away from the elements to store writing, drawing and other creative materials. But after that, it's often a case of rapidly diminishing returns. Stuff means work, and nowhere is this more true than in the case of houses.

Houses are the Godzilla of 'my life will be better when I have this'. The King Kong of 'people will think I'm not doing very well in life if I have a humble one'. The Colossus of possession-care. And the absolute Goliathon of expenditure. An average Australian home loan is for about $300,000. Add interest, and this means paying back around double that sum over a typical 25-year period. What's more, some recent studies into living environments have suggested that having a More Desirable Home has no apparent effect on overall happiness. So cross 'move to a better house' off your to-do list! Live in a cheap one and spend the money you've saved on working less, taking up skiing, or helping to bring back a rare parrot from the brink of extinction.

Your authors have experience of both renting and owning, and we are still very undecided as to whether the freedoms of renting are worth trading for the security of ownership, with all the responsibility it entails. For while the financial bondage of paying off a house might turn out to be worthwhile if you choose to sell it, the physical bondage to cleaning, organizing, upkeep, and the seemingly inevitable tendency to work endlessly on the thing to make it better, can *eat your life*.

As Frugal Hedonists we encourage and celebrate the urge to look after and cherish things, and improve them by creative and spirited labours. The only problem with applying this to houses, is that they are such *big* things. So maybe the best solution is to have much smaller houses. It certainly wouldn't be hard. Dwellings in Australia, America, and Canada have inflated so much over the last seventy years, that an average new home is now two to three times as big as those being built in most of Western Europe. The per-person floor space figures are equally staggering.

Changing concepts of an adequate family home

If your authors ever bought property with the idea of knocking down an existing house, it would almost certainly be for the purpose of building a *smaller* house and having a *larger* garden, rather than the other way round. Or we might build two small self-contained homes within a shared garden, and rent one out. Many of the factors that make small living spaces better for owning, apply equally well to renting: cheapness, lower heating and lighting costs, less to clean, less capacity for accumulating mountains of stuff that needs tending to, less room for comprehensive home entertainment systems that whittle away your impetus to go out into the world and engage…

There are myriad ways to live in a smaller space. Sharehousing, renting a bungalow in someone's backyard, building a little cabin on a block in the countryside, renting out half of the house you live in and own, moving to an apartment/unit/smaller house, or simply spending years travelling.

Whichever option you choose, it will naturally have a few minor inconveniences when compared to a multi-bedroom pad with masses of spare space. But along with the advantages we've cited above, it will also come with many less predictable perks. Like sharing resources with housemates and discovering stuff from them – be it a newfound love for indoor soccer or how to cook perfect poached eggs. Like having someone to look after your cat when you go away if you've got a bungalow-tenant in your backyard. Like doing more of your living in the garden because you *are* a bungalow tenant. Like being able to move your home to a new location whenever you please, or reach the leftover birthday cake in your mini-fridge from your sofa if you've built a 'tiny house' on a trailer-base (see our Further Resources section for more on the tiny house movement). Besides, given that the alternative is devoting the majority of your adult life to paying for, shopping for, and maintaining a building, not having that Perfect Space For Effortlessly Entertaining Up To Twelve Guests (which you end up using 1.73 times per year), is probably a worthwhile trade-off.

The Zen of non-renovation

In the olden days, people bought a house, fixed up any broken bits or peeling paint, and got on with life. Now, we renovate. Renovation (or 'remodeling', as it is known in the U.S.) has become a truly massive industry over the last two decades. Home improvement expenditure in America doubled between 1995 and 2013, despite the population only increasing by about one fifth. It has become the excuse for a lot of really over-zealous lifestyle television, and pretty much The Expected Thing To Do whenever you buy a building that is a little out of style or worn around the edges. Fixtures, finishes and floor plans that look dated have become unacceptable, no matter how serviceable. Renovating the house has become yet another task looming over people 'to get around to' as soon as they can find enough money or time. More than ever before, houses seem to be extensions of our self-image, and hence need grooming if we are not to feel badly about them.

Your authors have long regarded folk who don't care how their houses appear to other people as being somewhat enlightened – after all, there are infinitely more important things to be admired for than your style of accommodation. This gave us a revolutionary idea. It's not for everyone, but we're sure some people could take to it like liquid nails to a laminate-splashback. *Don't* renovate. As mentioned in the main part of this tip, a better home doesn't actually alter happiness levels, and just because something *can* be done, doesn't mean it *should* be done. Perhaps that house is just fine being imperfect. (See "25. Notice when you have enough" for more on this elevating ethos). Repair anything that's non-functional, or will cause more work later (like rusted gutters that let the rain sheet down your walls and rot the woodwork). Create atmosphere with lamps, favourite pictures, good cooking smells, music, maybe a lick of paint. Then accept the rest, and get back to all the other stuff the world has to offer. This approach has the gigantic advantage that you're unlikely to become overly precious about your domestic space, as so many people can't help but do once they've poured buckets of cash, sweat and tears into it.

DISCLAIMER: Annie once spent a whole week making sequined curtains and has absolutely no regrets. Your authors aren't condemning home beauti-fication, we just don't think you should do it to live up to anyone's standards but your own.

43. LET YOURSELF BE GROSSED OUT

ANYONE WHO'S BEEN DRAWN to pick up this book has likely felt a little grossed out by overconsumption at some point or another. There can indeed be something existentially depressing about gazing at the mountains of junk that spill out of people's garages, the endless TVs dumped on the street because people have upgraded to the latest model, the sight of someone stuffing a final few mouthfuls into a stomach already fit to burst before getting up from the restaurant table.

You might feel like a party pooper, but we say let this emotional tide rip: feeling disturbed is a natural, adaptive response to watching profligate resource use, and is a feeling worth heeding. Don't let it eat you up, just let it become a tool to help remind you how you *don't* want to operate.

44. ACCLIMATISE TO THE SEASONS

ACCLIMATISE MIGHT BE a bit of a banal word actually. Anticipate the coming of the seasons, then when they finally arrive, do little leaps of joy that you'd blush to be caught doing; gnash your teeth as you grow weary of their ways, then forgive them as you remind yourself of their distinct charms and their necessariness. Just don't try and ignore them or iron them out.

Annie remembers her geography teacher saying that much of culture is made by landscape – but what is landscape made by? Weather. And a bit of tectonic plate action. But a lot of weather. Weather carves earth over eons, and dresses it (or not) in vegetation and water bodies. Jungle vs. tundra, monsoon vs. blizzard; they may sound a bit like the fight listings in an entertainment wrestling spectacular, but they are grander than any such cultural blip – they are culture-*makers*. Give them some respect.

Weather should be one of the great flavour enhancers of life. If we heat and cool our buildings and cars to the same temperature year round, we deny ourselves this flavour – of snuggling into woolly jumpers and going a bit foetal on the couch with duvets and hot chocolate for entire evenings; of throwing the doors and windows open on the first proper spring day to let the smell of warming earth and jasmine rush in; of briny sweat licked from your upper lip as you demolish a slab of watermelon on a summer's afternoon.

In an ideal society your authors reckon we'd all down tools when the weather got too extreme. Half of what people complain about when temperatures get intense is the impossibility of *doing* anything: if sizzling heat became a cue to shut up schools and shops and swim or snooze or laze around languidly gossiping over an iced tea (or G&T), it might get more of a warm (ehem!) welcome. If the winter dark became a time for long evenings around fire-places telling stories, and ten-hour sleeps that let our bodies catch up on a bit of cellular repair and restocked us with dreams, it might be a yearned-for lull in the year rather than a dreaded ordeal.

Really want to save some pennies?

Do you realise quite how radiant you really are, precious reader? About as radiant as a 100 watt light globe – that's how much heat an average human body puts out while at rest. Add this to the heat generated by cooking and appliances (fridges, computers, lights), and in a mild climate, you can get a room pretty cosy over the course of a evening with all the doors and curtains kept snugly closed and a couple of people cooking dinner. If that's not enough, try putting on more clothing before even touching that temperature dial.

Meanwhile, letting your body adjust to the colder months speeds up your metabolism, so you burn off more calories while doing *nothing at all*. There should be an infomercial about it! Still, if it's a chilly evening and you want to *really* work on that physique, get up and do some push-ups every half an hour. The added bonus of getting toasty will put the pleasure back into pumping those pecs. The extra fitness will help your body better regulate its temperature too.

In the summer, keeping doors, windows and curtains closed during daylight hours (then throwing them open as soon as dusk arrives), sipping on icy drinks, and using a fan, can all keep you nice and cool for a tiny fraction of the energy costs of air conditioning.

Heating and air conditioning? Set the temperature to where you still feel a touch too warm or cool, and your body will adapt better to the season. Your pores contract in cold or dry weather so as to sweat less. It takes them a couple of weeks to get around to doing it properly, but they can't do it if you spend half your time in furnace-level temperatures. Your internal thermostat seems to adjust too: limit your use of heating and cooling, and although you'll gripe about the weather as much as anyone for the first few weeks of extreme temperatures, a month later, you might feel surprised to hear people talking about how unbearable it is. Obviously, this approach will also save you money.

When you eat seasonally your fruit bowl begins to look gratifyingly like the ones in medieval paintings.

Our second tenet of embracing seasonal contrast saves you money too. Buying fruit and vegetables that are out-of-season usually costs at least twice the in-season price. Seasonal eating also gets you fresher produce, which not only has better flavour and more of its nutritional properties intact, but does away with all that embodied energy of producing food in greenhouses or having it shipped from thousands of miles away where the weather is different. Wait for when the cherries start being sold by the box because the trees are so loaded with fruit – you might not want a whole box yourself, but use this as your heads-up that cherry season is truly here. In summer, look up five different recipes calling for lots of basil and zucchini (that's courgette to you Brits and Kiwis). Appreciate how the starchy tubers that store so well through winter also provide exactly the right ingredients for warming winter stews and mashes. Let yourself miss fresh tomatoes, knowing that the imported hydroponic ones sold in the cold months taste kind of like squeaky rubber dolphin bath toys anyway.

Here's a great recipe that uses seasonal abundance (basil, zucchini, and the delicious weed purslane all peak in production over the same period) and common garden herbs. We couldn't fit it into our *Weed Forager's Handbook*, so we're delighted to have an excuse to share it here.

Chilled Zucchini, Purslane and Basil Soup

   2 tablespoons good olive oil, plus extra for drizzling
   1 medium onion, chopped small
   2 garlic cloves, thinly sliced
   1 teaspoon thyme leaves
   1 bay leaf
   8 small zucchini (about 1¼ kgs), thinly sliced
   2 cups purslane (discard any large, tough stems – these can be pickled
       if you like)
   Salt to taste
   5 cups water
   3 tablespoons chopped basil
   Freshly ground pepper

1. In a large saucepan, heat the olive oil. Add the onion and garlic and salt and cook over moderate heat until soft and translucent. Stir in the thyme and bay leaf and cook until fragrant; about 1 minute. Add the sliced zucchini and the purslane, season with salt, and cook, stirring occasionally, until just tender; about 8 minutes. Add 3 cups of the water and bring to a boil, then remove the saucepan from the heat. Discard the bay leaf and stir in the basil. Add 2 cups of cold water, then allow the soup to cool a little further.

2. Puree the soup until very smooth. Refrigerate for at least 3 hours, until thoroughly chilled.

3. Season the soup with salt and pepper to taste. Ladle into shallow bowls and decorate with a few purslane sprigs and zucchini shavings if you like. Add a drizzle of olive oil and some cracked pepper and serve.

45. Some notes on style

"If our style is masterful ... we can live on top of content, float above the predictable responses, social programming and hereditary circuitry, letting the bits of colour and electricity and light filter up to us..."

~ Tom Robbins, *Another Roadside Attraction*

YOUR AUTHORS ARE BELIEVERS in style over substance being as legitimate an option as its more hallowed inverse. As Ella Fitzgerald sang: "It ain't what you do, it's the way that you do it". With some people, not caring an ounce about how they look is part of their charm. For these types, giving the finger to that particularly irksome facet of style that is appearance-maintenance, may even prove to be a frugality-compatible renaissance!

For others amongst us however, investing a little attention in looking dashing assists in conjuring the less definable aspects of personal style – how we move, the way we use our eyes and voices. We personally find that heeding this layer of being adds vitality and sauce to our lives. Presenting yourself with some panache can be an act of generosity too: most people get pleasure from physical spectacle, be it a scintillating colour combination, a spectacular beard, a walk with a panther-like grace, or an unchastened twinkle in the eyes.

Even though Pippi Longstocking inherited trunks of gold from her pirate
father she still understands that she looks more stylish in her mismatched
stockings and patchwork dress, because that's just the way she rolls.
Unfortunately copyright law prevents us from showing her outfit to you,
so here's a picture of her horse.

You may have guessed what's coming next – you *are* four fifths into the book
after all, and no one can be unpredictable *all* the time. Yep, we're going to
pronounce that frugality is no hindrance to style, and can even improve it!
Let's skip the part about how secondhand shops are a treasure trove of
individualistic fashion inspiration, as we're pretty sure even Oprah Winfrey
has done a special on the topic. For some thrifty connoisseurs of the closet,
the pre-loved clothing market will indeed be an invaluable ally, whether it be
charity shops, online trading, swaps with friends, or in the case of Adam's
handsomest shirt; finding clothes snagged on a bush by a country backroad
in a rainstorm (flawless 1200 thread count Ralph Lauren by the way…
Annie's eye spotted the quality flapping in the wind at fifty paces).

Dressing well is mostly about how you put things together anyway. If you
sew a little, or trade favours with a friend who does, you can make even more
out of the pieces that come your way. Add an occasional small item *a la mode*
into the mix to help give you that air of knowing what's what (if that's part

of what you're after). This is often a winning wardrobe strategy even for those who could afford to spend more – wearing a head to toe, up-to-the-minute outfit usually looks like you're trying way too hard. A similar kind of style downfall often also awaits those who overexert themselves on a gruelling regime of fake tanning, waxing, hair styling, endless gym sessions and mani-pedi's. These types can sometimes be spotted clacking along stiffly in an inelegance of demanding shoes and self-consciousness, eliciting derisive sniggers from the very people they had hoped to impress.

This is where the really extra special bonus for the Frugal Hedonist who cares about looks kicks in. Not only will you not look like you're trying too hard, but your very habits and mindset will tend to fit you out with erect bearing, an attractive physique, a mouth than doesn't slump at the corners, and a little fire in your eyes. No outfit looks as good without it.

The spunkiness of thriftiness

The science is in. Frugality is a *turn on*. It's not just because living less gluttonously keeps you lively and lithe. Show people identical photographs of a member of the opposite sex, then describe the subject of the photo in ways that portray them as either a 'saver' or 'spender'. Viewers will rate the same person's attractiveness quite differently depending on this description. You guessed it, frugalists – in a 2014 University of Michigan study – were considered 36% more attractive on average! According to the report, "savers are viewed as possessing greater general self-control, which increases both their romantic and physical attractiveness... Preference for savers was not influenced by participant age or relationship status, and it persisted when controlling for the participant's gender."

So, spending big on that first date could actually backfire. May we suggest instead, that you spice up the romance by requesting a take-home bag for your leftovers.

46. SAVE (ON) THE CHILDREN

YOUR AUTHORS ARE NOT PARENTS. We *have* spent a lot of time around kids, and one of us even worked professionally in childcare for several years, but we don't pretend to grasp the challenges of parenthood well enough to splash our own frugal child-raising ideas about in this book. Instead, we're choosing to consider the fact that we were raised frugally ourselves, and have many Frugal Hedonist friends who sport miniature sidekicks, as sufficient proof that children aren't an insurmountable barrier to living cheaply. We asked a selection of these friends about their top frugal-with-junior strategies. Here's what they came up with:

It pays to put in early effort. If there's ever a phase of life to free up as much time as you can – even if that means earning a pittance or letting the house go to pot – it's during your child's first five years. This is not so you have time to mollycoddle and hover over them. It is to allow you to spend a ridiculously long time making dinner, so that your child can help you with it and start building and enjoying kitchen skills. It's to leave you with enough energy to keep half an eye on them while they practise riding their tricycle up and down the sidewalk in the evening, rather than being so exhausted that you plonk them in front of a video instead. It's so you have time to look at advertisements with them and laugh at 'how crazy it is all the silly things people buy!' It is time to lie in the grass with them watching a trail of ants carrying huge crumbs, and let a little of their wonder rub off on you – and to show them by your pleasure at being there, that wonder is a worthwhile use of time. All this will help you wind up with a kid who is capable, hardy, and finds fun in creation as much as in consumption... making life cheaper and more relaxed in the long run.

Give your child a regular sum of spending money. Explain how they could use it to get some small things now, or to save for something bigger. Then let them make the choices. Increase the amount of money and what they are expected to buy for themselves out of it every year, adding a few more tips about budgeting each time. By the time they are teenagers, have them totally responsible for whole areas of their spending (for example, their clothing, entertainment and snacks budget). This gets kids thinking about ways to make that money go further, and teaches them appreciation for what they consume.

Spend as much time in natural and outdoor environments as possible. If you have a garden, make sure you leave a wild, unplanned area where kids can wreak their havoc without you getting stressed about it. Society teaches that happiness comes from 'getting', but nature-time helps kids realise that it also comes from 'doing', and even from just 'being'. Best of all, they will usually play independently for hours on end in such places, which is brilliant for your mental health.

If your child has grandparents, and you don't live near them, consider moving. Or beg them to move closer to you. Also, put as much energy as it takes into working out some good reciprocal childcare arrangements: one or two days a week, you mind a friend's child and they do the same for you (or increase this to three or four children who all play together well, rotating between several different houses throughout the week.) Also, maximize time where you hang out with several people and a pack of kids. The kids disappear into their own universe of play, and only come interrupt the adult fun if they've grazed their knee. A perk of both these set-ups is that kids have to figure out how to get along with different ages and genders, whereas at childcare centres or schools they often end up in homogenous little cliques.

Avoid making them special food. They eat what you eat, maybe minus the chilli sauce. If they refuse to eat it, don't fret, they won't starve. Involving them in cooking food makes kids much more inclined to eat it, and regularly eating together helps them to respect and enjoy food and to learn basic operation of a knife and fork by imitating you.

Make rules, have expectations. You and this small person have to create a functional life together, or you will end up feeling browbeaten. Make it clear that you will simply never buy candy from a supermarket checkout, no matter how big the tantrum. Make it clear that of course they will join in with doing the housework every Saturday morning – involve them in discussing what chores might be best to have as their special jobs, and also in discussing what fun thing you'll do every week when you're finished. Don't praise them for abiding by these expectations (although do praise a job well-done), but make it clear how disappointed you are if they don't fulfil them.

Be clear and give reasons. When you say 'No' (…we are not going to buy that toy) or 'You have to' (…brush your teeth even though you don't feel like it), say it with certainty, and also briefly explain why. Introduce this important concept: 'In life there's always some things that we don't like, but that have to be the way they are. But there are always millions of things to like at the same time, so it's silly to waste energy making a big stink over the bits we don't like, because then we'd have no energy left to enjoy all the good bits.' Your job is not to create a being who never suffers, because that's unrealistic. It's to create one who deals gracefully with suffering when it comes along, and gets the most out of everything in between.

Go for frugal forms of entertainment. Make use of some of the zillions of free kids' activities to be found in most large cities, especially during school holidays – from museums to story hours at the local library to discovery trails in the botanic garden. At home, keep animals, even if it's just mice, and give the kids some of the responsibility for looking after them. Tell stories, do drawings, wrestle, go foraging. Let them get bored, because that's when they learn to be creative about entertaining themselves. Teach them the fun of finding, fixing and re-appropriating old stuff. Get them involved in anything useful you're doing; children love to feel like they're doing grown-up things! And don't forget how often what you enjoyed doing most as a kid didn't involve any adults. So leave them alone. To puddle about in water and dirt, sing made-up songs, play dress-ups, and invent imaginary worlds.

Expect phases. Once kids start trying to define their own identity within society and their peer group, buying stuff often becomes a tool they want to use to help with this process. Firstly, remind yourself that in hindsight most people reflect on having been brought up frugally as a really good thing – so even though your child may be convinced that they are suffering unbearable deprivation right now, that feeling is unlikely to last. Secondly, if you do end up making some concessions at this point, don't beat yourself up about it: parenting is tough enough as it is. Thirdly, if you are feeling horrified by the consumption-crazed demon you appear to have spawned, comfort yourself with the fact that you have taught your offspring to be questioning and thoughtful by discussing things with them. You've modelled the values you'd like them to have, so they will be pretty likely to turn into a good adult once they find their feet.

Finally, use having kids as a *reason* to be more Frugally Hedonistic. They make you look at the world with freshly wonderous eyes, and are themselves utterly fascinating creatures worth being in the moment for, so you're already part way there. They also make a mockery out of any attempts to pursue material perfection, so that's handy.

On a whole different note, everyone should feel okay about questioning whether they want to reproduce at all, and if so, how many times. Obviously it's a whole different ballgame from deciding whether to buy a new car or not, but the pressure to have a child, or to have a second one to 'keep the first one company', can have something in common with the social pressures surrounding other lifestyle expectations. It's a terrible state of affairs that in an era of overpopulation people are made to feel defensive about not having children. If it is a real yearning in your heart of hearts, that's one story. But if it ain't, there are plenty of other amazing life experiences to have, and ways to contribute to the world.

47. Don't give up just because you gave in

DARLING READER, we are very much for the rampant enjoying of things, and not that interested in self-flagellation. We think it's good policy to stick with this approach even if you have a frugal blowout. A slightly ironic bonus of being a Frugal Hedonist is that if you *do* occasionally find yourself with an extravagant consumption craving, and you size it up and decide to go for it, you get to do it without the post-spending regret that eats at so many people. After all, it's a rare event, and both your bank balance and waistline (imagining it's a hot fudge sundae you're yearning for) are in fine fettle.

Curiously, we've also found that if you size up your craving and then decide instead to make it disappear in a puff of smoke using only the power of your mind, it feels almost like a magic trick, and is pretty much as fantastic as giving in.

48. Bow down before the nanna and get ahead of the curve

ONE STEREOTYPE of *dysfunctional* frugalism is the elderly person who grew up before material excess became the norm, and to this day saves teabags for repeated uses, repairs plastic bags with sticky tape, and washes their hair with vinegar.

They lived through times in which that was highly functional behaviour, particularly if they are old enough to remember the Great Depression. But by retaining such habits into an age of abundance, they attract patronising smiles, and even ridicule.

In these pages your authors have not lingered long on ethical or environmental reasons for being frugal. We started writing this book because people kept asking us how we seemed to always be having such a good time while saving so much money, and it struck us as a question worth answering. But it is also one that will likely become increasingly important into the future. For it seems probable at this point that population growth, resource constraints, and a shaky global economy will soon put pressure on most of us to consume less. In many cases, much, much less.

So isn't it possible that there might occur a flipping of the Pancake of Scorn? That profligacy may replace frugality as the embarrassingly outdated mode?

Attempting to hold onto high-consumption, wasteful behaviours into a future where they are increasingly acknowledged as dysfunctional would likely earmark people for ridicule. Or worse. The adjectives associated with overconsumption – greedy, spoilt, selfish, piggy – are sharper barbs than any reserved for the intensely frugal. An era of resource constraints is an era where it is more evident that one person's wastage is another's want. So living in constant excess might make you decidedly unpopular.

Trending: already unpopular and only likely to get more so...

~ People who run air conditioning 24/7 in summer, meaning passers-by (who aren't using any fossil fuel themselves, given that they are walking down the street rather than driving in a temperature-controlled car) get blasted with an extra gust of heat coming out of each aircon vent. These people also raise the temperature of the whole area for everyone else.

~ People who drive their kids back and forth to school in huge SUVs (rather than walking, riding, or carpooling in a reasonable vehicle), using up our dwindling oil supplies for the convenience, blowing fumes into the faces of every cyclist sitting behind them in traffic, and meaning that by the time we are all old there might be no way to boil a kettle for a cuppa apart from chopping wood to make a fire.

~ People who accept plastic cutlery, bags and cardboard carry trays for their plastic and paper containers of takeaway food and drink, and then cram the whole lot in a bin after eating from it for ten minutes, meaning that none of us will have the simple luxury of highly functional plastic objects (like buckets, or sealable food containers) for as long into the future. Or for that matter, the pleasure of looking at forested landscapes, rather than rubbish dumps.

If such a shift is to occur, it certainly seems most elegant to do what humans do so astonishingly well, and adapt, rather than clinging to old habits in petulant denial. The bonus here is, dear reader, that you and your Frugally Hedonistic friends, with your twinkly eyes, your bag of skills, and your ability to take maximum pleasure in words and weather, will have the jump on the situation! You may have to deal with neighbours clamouring for advice on how to grow pumpkins or fix a stereo system, but you'll be less likely to be traumatised by having to walk back from the shops carrying your groceries in a backpack. And less likely to end up sleeping in your car in a recession. (And even if you do, you'll have a better chance of knowing how to keep yourself healthy and happy while you're doing it!)

So don't pooh-pooh the habits of different eras. Bow down before the frugal nanna! Bring the oldest person you know a hot beverage, and ask them how they made things work in times of scarcity. Ask them what made them happy, hopeful and strong when they had next to nothing. Ask them what was good about it. They know how much things can change within a lifetime, and they might just be able to help you understand how much flexibility this requires. And how much we are capable of.

We did press Nesta, our one remaining grandma, for a quote on this subject. However, she's more into cigarettes, gossip, and spoiling terriers silly, than analysing how she has managed to convey such a lifelong air of glamour and decadence while generally spending a pittance.

49. GIVE SOMETHING

WHETHER IT'S MONEY, help, time, or things, giving asserts that you have enough to spare, which keeps you from conning yourself into a mindset of not having enough. Which helps you feel sleek and satiated within your frugality. *And* it helps other people. Genius.

In fact, it's a neat little circle of win-win, what with being frugal meaning you end up with more to give, and giving helping you to be a more contented frugalist. Giving doesn't necessarily mean soup kitchens or Oxfam, it could mean spending more time listening to and caring for a frail or lonely family member, or taking the extra time to drop excess garden produce around to neighbours. Or dedicating as much effort as is needed to help a friend through a long dark tunnel of the soul. You have more energy left for this stuff when you're not frazzled by forty-hour weeks and a flotilla of credit card debts.

Some people find that giving away actual cold hard cash keeps them honest in their assessment of how much of it they really need (and how comparatively rich they really are). Adam has a friend who is a simple-living, intrepid-travelling mathematics lecturer who regards the salary he receives as an accidental reflection of an unfairly distorted economy. Every second paycheck goes into a bank account for a school in India that he helped establish. He says, "It isn't my money the way I look at it, so how can I keep it? I don't want it – I'd have to find a satisfying means of spending it. In my context that might mean going on a big long trip, but I do that anyway. What else would I do with it? Look for a fancy new blender? If I had lots of money I'd have to think about how to manage it best, and I don't want to have to think about that."

Giving is the best medicine

Mark Twain once said, "The best way to cheer yourself up is to try to cheer somebody else up" which your authors reckon makes total sense, given that you have to step outside your own self-critical internal monologue and really pay attention to someone to cheer them up. Volunteering in the community, or simply providing support to family and friends, has in fact been shown to correlate with increased longevity, decreased distress, and increased feelings of meaning. A University of California study found that volunteering for at least two organizations was as beneficial as exercising four times a week in terms of reducing mortality rates. One study in the 1980s even found that just *watching* Mother Teresa do charitable things increased onlookers' immune system antibodies. In several studies, results indicated that caring for or spending money on others conferred more health and happiness benefits than being cared for or spending money on yourself.

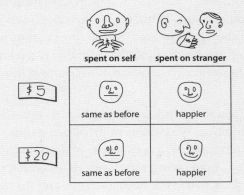

Students were given envelopes with either $5 or $20 in them, and instructions to either spend it on themselves or on a stranger (such as treating a stranger to a cup of coffee). The next day, those that spent the money on a stranger reported feeling happier, whereas those that spent it on themselves felt no different (regardless of how much money they were given).

50. SUP AT THE CULTURAL BUFFET

CULTURAL BACKLASHES HAVE A WAY of oversteering. There was a lot to dislike about being a peasant, to be sure. Think superstitions, thatched roofs, hair lice, and 17th century dentistry. But as the potential for being middle class emerged, we may have gotten a tad overexcited, and ditched all manner of very worthwhile peasanty things in our enthusiasm. Take, for instance, growing food at home. What might the neighbours say?! "Can't you afford food from the supermarket?" So the rise of suburbia last century saw everyone who was anyone ditching the vegetable patch and cultivating a patch of lawn instead; previously an ostentatious status symbol reserved for the English gentry.

Now we're at a point where the industrial middle class experiment has been running for few generations. We citizens of privileged nations have immersed ourselves in home entertainment, a cornucopia of domestic appliances, interior design, bottled Fijian spring water, supermarket shopping and life coaches. Who could deny that it has been a strange and marvellous ride? But one dense with inane and passive thrills, giving us short attention spans, huge rates of legal and illegal drug use for anxiety and depression, youth suicide, obesity, existential crises and so many distracting cute animal YouTube videos that it's hard to get on with having a life. (Although – have you seen that one where the cheeky gibbon pinches teenage tigers on the ears? Because that's almost worth not having a life for.)

But we digress. The point your authors would like to make is that it would be silly for a Frugal Hedonist to be disdainful of everything associated with middle class living and modern technologies – to repeat the mistake we all made when we rejected peasant culture in such a wholesale fashion. The luxury of history is that we can survey what has and hasn't worked out well for various incarnations of humankind, and adopt a cultural mash-up approach accordingly.

Adam corresponded for some time with a well-travelled West Papuan tribesman who said the only thing he liked about the modern world was the internet. We're not quite so extreme. We'd add to the list: recorded music, lightweight tents, stick mixers, strings of little coloured lights, bicycles, occasional air travel, and sneakers. And from other eras we'll take physically active lifestyles, space for luxuriant contemplation and conversation, knowing how to recognize food in the landscape, time without screens, and finding quiet grassy hollows to take a nap in with your head resting in the crook of your arm. Amongst other things.

Make your own list. Really assess what you think works and is worthwhile in modern culture, and what you think other times and other peoples did better (or were better off without). Think about creating a chimera life based on your evaluation. Maybe you'll move to a tiny apartment, get rid of your TV, take up letter writing and amateur circus in the evenings, and spend six months of every year bicycle touring with a bag of oats in your pannier and the best lightweight rain gear technology can supply. Maybe you'll become a modern monk-scholar who spends your days in deep reverent study at a warm, well-lit library, and your nights helping to feed the hungry from a soup van, before skateboarding home on the quiet midnight freeways, nibbling on feral-goat jerky. We'd like to have some home-grown dandelion coffee with you in our kitchen decorated with golden glitter while listening to Scandinavian synth pop on our solar powered laptop when you do…

51. Look up, think about constellations. Look down, think about magma.

Sometimes when you are feeling drenched by the details of your own life, it's time to pack a suitcase for your myopia, and send it on holiday.

Look up. There is so infinitely much more matter than you out there, hurling forth glowing plumes, imploding into vortexes, converging into gaseous balls, then shattering into incandescent rain. It is endless and eternal and entropic and generative and holy in the most religion-irrelevant sense of the word.

Look down. There is the great grinding, shifting, melting foundry for all the yawning canyons and toothed peaks and rift valleys. There is the alchemical trinity of moisture, mineral, and organic debris that has the power to birth new life, and which informs the composition of your bones, the structure of your extracellular matrix, the very viscosity of your blood.

Remembering where and what you are should not be to the end of feeling like an insignificant speck. You are woven of this stuff, this starlight and magma, let it extend you and make you feel endless amongst it, swathed in the vastness of time, rich in your very elemental connectedness. *Then* scan what feels important to you as a creature.

Annie says it's moving with panache, grinning slightly crazily, watching animals running, making out, feeling sun and water on her skin, anything that sparkles, panting and sweating, dreaming, and eye contact. Adam says it's letting himself vibrate with a gargantuan awareness of all the impressiveness and fuckedupness, and of being a player in an unfolding story of quite dramatic proportions (the one about the naked apes that discovered fossil fuels and created a global civilisation with genetic engineering and music made by people trying to sound like robots).

It's not as if you can keep this stuff in mind all the time. But make a nook in your brain that remembers it, and you can step into it whenever you want to put things back in perspective. Going there can give you giant feelings zizzing through your body. It is also likely to make you feel less needy, and maybe even a bit euphoric.

Sounds a bit like being a Frugal Hedonist.

FURTHER RESOURCES

Lifestyles, real and imagined, to help you recalibrate

Tales from the Green Valley (Lion Television for BBC Two, 2005). A team of historians and archaelogists recreate the lifestyle of a 1620s Welsh farm for a year and, and as hard as it is, they kind of love it. In fact, they must have really loved it, as several of them went on to do series set in the rural lifestyles of several other eras. Annie wants to come clean: she has watched every one of these series, some of them more than once.

Entropia by Samuel Alexander (The Simplicity Institute, 2013). Someone had to be brave enough to write it: not so much a novel as an attempt at envisaging of what a sustainable society might look like.

The Transition movement is a global network of people creating whole streets and towns that are moving to a lower-energy use, more community-based lifestyle. Their website is dense with resources. www.transitionnetwork.org.

Welcome to Lagos (BBC, 2010). An excellent three part miniseries about how people make do in the slums of Lagos, Nigeria. Makes you feel spoilt rotten, grateful, and inspired all at once.

The Supersizers Go... Wartime (Series 1, episode 1. BBC Two, 2008). Two food obsessed Britons eat a diet from the ration books of World War 2. Because they're comedians, they have to make lots of 'blech' noises while eating the austere diet, but because they are comedians, it is also hilarious, and there's interesting stuff to take away about how during wartime people got healthier, social bonds got stronger, and treats felt... treatier.

Animal, Vegetable, Miracle by Barbara Kingsolver. (HarperCollins 2007) Kingsolver's genius is her ability to take what could seem to some like threateningly left-wing-greenie values, and present them in a way that makes apparent how much they have in common with classic conservative values: self reliance, thrift, strong family and community bonds. This book charts her family's year of trying to eat almost exclusively off of their farm. Her novels are worth reading too, and tend to cleverly wrap staggering ecological questions up in what can at first glance seem like easily digestible airport fiction.

The Woodsman's Cottage (series 9, episode 13, of *Grand Designs*. Fremantle Media, 2003). Several people have mentioned to us how much this story affected them. It's about a British woodsman who, after 10 years living under canvas in the woods waiting for planning permission, builds a stunningly handmade home.

Possum Living by Dolly Freed (Universe Books, 1978). Written by a 19-year-old firecracker. Dolly explains "how to be lazy, proud, miserly, and honest, live well and enjoy leisure." We don't agree with a bunch of things she says, and some of her advice wouldn't work in this era, but there's buckets of infectious attitude, plus lots of self-sufficiency tips of the how-to-skin-a-rabbit variety.

Questioning culture

Affluenza: When Too Much is Never Enough by Clive Hamilton and Richard Denniss (Allen & Unwin, 2005). A definitive and damning overview of overconsumption in modern Australia, packed with jaw-dropping figures illustrating our ballooning consumption expectations. Also looks at changes that could get things back on track, both political and personal. (There is also an American book and related documentary, both called Affluenza, that deal with the ill effects of overconsumption in a more comedic style. Although now a tad dated, their content is still totally relevant.)

📖 *Plenitude: The New Economics of True Wealth* by Juliet Schor (Penguin Press HC, 2010). An in-depth look at how the current economic model is fated, and how we could restructure labour and leisure to create one that isn't. Makes particularly interesting points about how much of growth is illusory.

📖 *Religion for Atheists: A Non-believer's Guide to the Uses of Religion* by Alain de Botton (2012). A fascinating investigation of how religion uses rituals and regular revisiting of many forms of emblematic art (from architecture to literature to music to painting) to help remind followers of how they want to behave and who they aspire to be. The book then makes a case for using the same devices in secular society to make it easier for us to stay true to our best visions of ourselves in the face of petty distractions.

🎥 *The Lightbulb Conspiracy* (written and directed by Cosima Dannoritzer, 2010). Documentary focussing on planned obsolescence, and other unpleasant aspects of how companies keep us buying as much as possible for as long as possible. If you had any doubts about the sheer rotten-ness of big business, this will cure you of them.

Money

📖 *Your Money or Your Life: 9 Steps to Transforming Your Relationship with Money and Achieving Financial Independence* by Vicki Robin and Joe Dominguez (Penguin, 2008) is an American book written to help you do an intensive life-audit so you can figure out where to downshift most usefully. Even if you don't want to put your finances and values through the book's nine-step evaluation program, reading all the in-between bits about true hourly wages and contradictions between what we really want and how we spend is still worthwhile.

📖 *Happy Money: The Science of Smarter Spending* by Elizabeth Dunn and Michael Norton (Simon & Schuster, 2013) is a research-based tour of spending, presenting five main ways we can change our spending to makes ourselves happier. Very clever, potentially life-changing.

👆 **Centre for Effective Altruism** helps you figure out how to best give money away. www.centreforeffectivealtruism.org. One of their projects, Giving What You Can, features a **'How Rich Am I?'** calculator, which is good for bringing home how wealthy you are relative to the average earth denizen: www.givingwhatwecan.org/get-involved/how-rich-am-i

Work... and not doing as much of it

📖 *How to Be Idle: A Loafer's Manifesto* by Tom Hodgkinson (Harper Perennial, 2007) is a charismatic and rambling incitement to do less, loaded with encouraging historical examples and quotes from laziness-loving luminaries of literature and philosophy.

👆 **The New Economics Foundation: 21 Hours:** www.neweconomics.org/publications/entry/21-hours. It is also worth heading back to the NEF home page and checking out the whole website.

👆 **Centre for a New American Dream** looks at the benefits of a shorter work week in a set of beautifully clear infographics. www.newdream.org/resources/infographics-shorter-workweek. Again, this whole site has loads of good stuff.

Food

📖 *Frugavore* by Arabella Forge (Skyhorse Publishing, 2011) is a great breakdown of how eating tastier, more nutritious food can actually be cheaper when you do it right – includes recipes.

📖 Michael Pollan's suite of food-related books *The Omnivore's Dilemma, In Defence of Food, Food Rules, Cooked* (all published by Penguin) are great for getting you fired up abut really appreciating what you eat.

📖 *The Art of Fermentation* by Sandor Katz (Chelsea Green, 2012) is the bible of fermentation. Fermentation can be a beautiful alchemy of extending a food's shelf life while turning it into something more delicious (and full of probiotics).

The Weed Forager's Handbook by your authors, Adam Grubb and Annie Raser-Rowland (Hyland House, 2013) is a guide to spotting and eating edible wild herbs. It's Australian focused, but applicable to many of the planet's temperate areas. You will also find many photos of edible weeds at the accompanying website: www.eatthatweed.com

Putting Food By by Ruth Hertzberg, Janet Greene and Beatrice Vaughan (Plume, 2010) is a classic guide to bottling, canning, drying, freezing and pickling.

There's a lot of blogs out there that give suggestions for how to **cook with limited ingredients**, use up leftovers, what to freeze and not freeze etc. Here's one that includes a bundle of useful info: www.thestonesoup.com

Permablitz is an international collective that does backyard make-overs... permaculture style. Volunteers give their time helping to 'blitz' one garden into a productive paradise in exchange for onsite learning and the option to have their own gardens permablitzed. www.permablitz.net

The Art and Science of Dumpster Diving by John Hoffman (Breakout Productions, 1992). He doesn't pull any punches, and touches on just about every form of dumpster diving there is. Takes more of an 'each man for himself' attitude than your authors would like to see in the dumpstering world.

Housing

A good website about **tiny houses**: www.thetinylife.com

House sitting. There are local networks for this, so just do an internet search for your city's name plus 'house sitting'.

Retrofitting. This Australian governmental site focuses on different aspects of sustainable building. It includes information on retrofitting existing homes for improved energy efficiency, incorporating several detailed case studies. www.yourhome.gov.au

Personal transport

👆 **Car-sharing**. There are lots of different car-sharing networks, but no great central directory we could find. So your best bet is an internet search for 'car-sharing' and your city's name. There are two different models: the standard business model one, where the fleet of cars are distributed throughout the suburbs, but are owned centrally by a company (in 'Self-propel' we mentioned the U.S. example of Zipcar, www.zipcar.com); and the peer-to-peer model, where people in the neighbourhood lease their personal car (we mentioned an Australian example: Car Next Door, www.carnextdoor.com.au).

👆 **Car-pooling**. There are car-pooling or ride-sharing networks for sharing car *journeys*. Traditionally car-pooling has been used for prearranging sharing petrol costs over longish journeys or for regular commutes to work and back. Recently smartphone technologies are opening up possibilities for more spontaneous journeys, and taxi-like distances, known as real-time ride-sharing.

An example of the former model is www.eRideShare.com, and of the latter, the US-based, www.lyft.com or the Australian www.coseats.com. But again, you're best off doing an internet search to find your local ones.

Travel

📓 *The Art of Free Travel: A Frugal Family Adventure* by Patrick Jones and Meg Ulman (New South Books, 2015). As mentioned in 'Have a lot of things you want to do with your liberty'

👆 **Couchsurfing** is a network of people that let travellers stay with them. Hosting other travellers makes hosts more likely to host you when you're travelling. www.couchsurfing.org

👆 **WWOOF** (Willing Workers on Organic Farms) is a loose network of organisations that connect travellers with hosts. Travellers can exchange farm work for food and board. Find regional networks at: www.wwoof.net

👆 **HelpX** (www.helpx.net) and **Workaway** (www.workaway.info) are similar networks to WWOOF, but also list properties that have nothing to do with farming or gardening. So if you can't schlep a shovel, you can find places looking for builders, babysitters, language practice, etc. They also have the advantage of online systems to rate and review hosts.

☝ **Warm Showers** is kind of like Couchsurfing for cycle tourists. www. warmshowers.org

☝ **House-swaps**. For longer stays you can often get free accommodation, sometimes in return for taking care of pets etc. One website is: www.homeexchange.com

☝ It's pretty famous. **Airbnb** is a place where people rent out accommodation, including their houses while they're away. It caters to a wide range of budgets. www.airbnb.com

☝ **Hitchhiking** is one of our favourite ways of getting around. This page (on **Wikitravel** – a great collaborative source of free travel information) is full of excellent tips: www.wikitravel.org/en/Tips_for_hitchhiking.
Hitchwiki is full of user-generated info with town-by-town tips and interactive maps on hitching points and experience. www.hitchwiki.org

☝ **Sleeping in Airports** is a user-generated guide to – as you may have inferred – sleeping in airports. www.sleepinginairports.net

Sharing and free things

☝ **StreetBank** is a website for sharing tools and other things with neighbours. www.streetbank.com

☝ **TuShare** is kind of like an eBay of free stuff (Australian only). Lots of books, clothes and furniture. www.tushare.com

☝ **Freecycle** is a network of local groups where people offer free stuff they don't want anymore. www.freecycle.org

Fixing stuff / making stuff

👆 **Instructables** has absolutely thousands of DIY projects and repairs, with everything from face cream recipes to tractor repairs. www.instructables.com

👆 **iFixit** is an online community of people helping each other fix stuff. Small in scale, but growing. www.ifixit.com

👆 **Repair Café** is a global network of meeting places where you can find tools and get help fixing your broken stuff – they started in Amsterdam, and there are now over 750 of them, though only a few in Australia at this stage. www.repaircafe.org

Random fascinating

📖 *Paradox of Choice* by Barry Schwartz (Ecco, 2003). Very interesting look at how too much consumer choice makes us unhappy.

📖 *The Power of Habit Why We Do What We Do in Life and Business* by Charles Duhigg. Eminently readable book about the nuts and bolts of habit formation. Although some chapters of this book are geared towards improving business practice, it also offers many useful clues as how to give personal habits a makeover.

📖 *The Happiness Hypothesis* by Jonathon Haidt (Basic Books, 2006). Fantastic book on the science of happiness.

Source material

We owe a great gratitude to all the makers who release their material free for reuse under Creative Commons licences. Those we've used are listed below. Unless listed, the images in this book are either our own, or in the public domain.

Have a lot of things you want to do with your freedom
The photo of the Artist as Family is reprinted with kind permission from Meg Ulman and Patrick Jones.

Recalibrate your senses
Photo of the aeroplane licensed under CC BY-SA 3.0 by Arcturus at commons.wikimedia.org.

Stop reading those magazines
The facial expressions photos are cropped from:
Face 1: CC BY-SA 2.0 by Andy Miah on flickr.com.
Face 3: CC BY 2.0 by Tony Crescibene on flickr.com.

Romanticise other eras
The quote from MATILDA by Roald Dahl is copyright © 1988 by Roald Dahl. Used by permission of Viking Children's Books, an imprint of Penguin Young Readers Group, a division of Penguin Random House LLC for the US and Canada, and by Jonathan Cape Ltd and Penguin Books Ltd for the rest of the world.

Enjoy excess
La Tomatina photo licensed CC BY 2.0 by Graham McLellan at flickr.com.

Listen to the habit scientists
Bodybuilder photo licensed CC BY-SA 3.0 by Dalston at sk.wikipedia.org.

Find free third places
Public square photo licensed CC BY-SA 3.0 by Nsaum75 at en.wikipedia.org.

Grow your own greens
Giant tortoise photo licensed CC BY-SA 2.0 by 5of7 at flickr.com.

Indulge your curiosity
Baby ladybird photo licensed CC BY-SA 3.0 by Alpsdake at commons.wikimedia.org.

Don't be a selfish %$*#
Alps photo licensed CC BY-SA 4.0 by Martin Steiger at commons.wikimedia.org.

Reinvent Christmas
'Typical American Christmas scene' photo licensed CC BY-SA 2.0 by Kim Love at flickr.com. Cupcake photo licensed CC BY-SA 3.0 by Bugeater3 at commons.wikimedia.org.

People who need people are the luckiest people in the world
Bust of Epicurus photo licensed CC BY 2.5 by Marie-Lan Nguyen at commons.wikimedia.org.

Undercomplicate things
Prince Charles photo licensed CC BY-SA 2.0 by Revolve Eco-Rally at flickr.com.

Self-propel
Credit for the data for the Houston carpark image goes to photoLith at forum.skyscraperpage.com (which we were able to check the accuracy of using Google street view). Bicyclist photo licensed CC BY 3.0 by Jean-Marie Hullot at fotopedia.com.

Have less house
Cottage photo licensed CC BY-SA 2.0 by Jocelyn Kinghorn at flickr.com. Big house photo licensed CC BY-SA 3.0 by WikiCats at en.wikipedia.org.

Some notes on style
Sitting horse in the Pippi's horse montage licensed CC BY 2.0 by Jean (7326810@N08) at flickr.com.

Bow down before the nanna and get ahead of the curve
The photo of grandmother Nessie is by Ben Grubb.

Key to licences
CC BY = Creative Commons Attribution
CC BY-SA = Creative Commons Attribution-Share Alike
Full information at www.creativecommons.org

Author bios

ANNIE RASER-ROWLAND

Annie may write 'horticulturalist' when she fills out the Main Occupation box on her tax return, but she considers herself an aesthete first and foremost. (She also usually writes some very small numbers in the Earnings box, yet considers herself incredibly rich.) She takes immense pleasure in the sensual world, and sees enjoying it without destroying it to be her main aim as a human being. She's keen to help others do the same, and gave up making art in favour of teaching people how to feed themselves sustainably. She has worked on permaculture projects in far-flung countries, co-authored with Adam *The Weed Forager's Handbook: A Guide to Edible and Medicinal Weeds in Australia*, and taught workshops and given innumerable people advice on keeping little green caterpillars away from broccoli in her role at CERES Environmental Park's nursery in Melbourne. In between, she finds mountain ranges to walk up and down, draws pictures of her dog, and lies in her local park reading detective novels and eating home-grown bananas in the sunshine.

ADAM GRUBB

Adam has voluntarily spent much of his adult life as a frugalist, including stretches spending radically tiny amounts – think under $2000 annually. He loves the challenge. What's more, it gives him time to do unpaid work, such as the years he spent founding the energy news website EnergyBulletin.net (now Resilience.org). He's also one of the co-founders of the global permablitz movement of volunteer-executed garden makeovers, and has a weekly radio show called Greening the Apocalypse on Melbourne's Triple R. For money, he is a permaculture designer and educator in his business Very Edible Gardens in Melbourne, Australia, which he codirects with Dan Palmer. Plus he lets Annie cajole him into writing books with her sometimes.

The Weed Forager's Handbook: A Guide to Edible and Medicinal Weeds in Australia

by Adam Grubb and Annie Raser-Rowland

Step into the world of our least-admired botanical companions, peel back the layers of prejudice, and discover the finer side of the plants we call weeds. An astonishing number are either edible or medicinal, and have deep and sometimes bizarre connections to human history.

But how do you distinguish a tasty sandwich-filler from its dangerous look-alike?

Which of these garden familiars is the most nutritious vegetable ever tested by the US Department of Agriculture?

How do you cook with delicious nettles without fear of being stung?

This book reveals all this and more, and will forever change your concept of where to go looking for lunch.

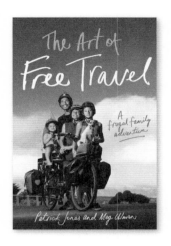

THE ART OF FREE TRAVEL: A FRUGAL FAMILY ADVENTURE

by Patrick Jones and Meg Ulman

Patrick, Meg and their family had built a happy, sustainable life. But in late 2013, they found themselves craving adventure: a road trip.

But theirs was a road trip with a difference. With Zephyr (10), Woody (1) and their dog, they set off on a year-long cycling journey along Australia's east coast, from Daylesford to Cape York and back.

Their aim was to live cheap – guerrilla camping, hunting and foraging. They spent time in Aboriginal communities, joined an anti-fracking blockade, documented edible plants, and dodged speeding trucks on the country's most dangerous highways. *The Art of Free Travel* is the remarkable story of a rule-breaking year of ethical living.

Permaculture Pioneers: Stories from the New Frontier

edited by Caroline Smith and Kerry Dawborn

These compelling stories describe how ordinary people found the courage to embrace the world's problems and move beyond fear to make a difference and empower others with solutions and practical actions, as inspired agents of change.

This anthology is an inspiring addition to permaculture publications, and of interest to anyone concerned with social and environmental change.

One of the book's key messages is that everyday folk do not have to wait for experts and governments to lead. The experiences of the Permaculture Pioneers illustrate that we can all be courageous and creative. We all have the tools to empower ourselves, rather than simply being dragged along in a flow we feel we cannot escape.

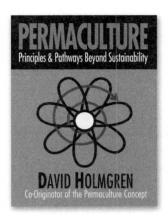

PERMACULTURE:
PRINCIPLES AND PATHWAYS
BEYOND SUSTAINABILITY

by David Holmgren

Permaculture co-originator David Holmgren's seminal work, *Principles and Pathways* draws together and integrates 25 years of thinking and teaching to show a whole new way of understanding and performing a simple set of design principles.

Relevant to every aspect of how we reorganise our lives, communities and landscapes to creatively adapt to ecological realities which shape human destiny.

For the general reader this book provides refreshing perspectives on a range of environmental issues and shows how permaculture is much more than a system of gardening. For anyone seriously interested in understanding the foundations for sustainable design and culture, this book is essential reading.

AVAILABLE FROM HOLMGREN.COM.AU

RetroSuburbia: A Downshifter's Guide to a Resilient Future

by David Holmgren

RetroSuburbia explains and illustrates patterns, designs and behavioural strategies applied by those already on the downshifting path to a resilient future, using permaculture ethics and principles.

It offers design solutions to problems faced by those applying a more systematic, whole-of-household approach to retrofitting their homes, gardens and living arrangements.

It includes some proven design specifications and pointers, references technical sources and case studies, but is more of a strategic guide than a technical manual.

For more about this title visit RetroSuburbia.com